BOI

A Muddlebay Mystery

Book 1

by

Wendy Cartmell

This edition published 2021.
ISBN: 9798700928045
Imprint: Independently published
by Costa Press

By Wendy Cartmell

Sgt Major Crane crime thrillers:

Crane and Anderson crime thrillers:

Emma Harrison mysteries

Supernatural suspense

All my books are in KINDLE UNLIMITED and available to purchase or borrow from Amazon by clicking the covers.

Chapter 1

As soon as Flynn Moran saw DCI Wright, he knew something was wrong. Flynn had been summoned to the chief's office, which was an unusual occurrence in itself. Flynn couldn't image what the boss wanted. As he waited, with some trepidation, he noticed DCI Wright's normally calm features seemed strained. He was peering at Flynn closely, where normally he'd ignore him as much as possible, and Flynn could hear the man's foot tapping under his desk. Flynn wondered what was wrong with the boss. Stress? Some trouble at home perhaps?

'Well, Flynn,' he said.

'Yes, I am, thank you,' Flynn replied politely.

DCI Wright briefly closed his eyes and then opened them, looking at Flynn as though he were a species he'd not come across before. Flynn found it very disconcerting, this close scrutiny, but managed to keep looking at the chief instead of the floor. He wondered if there was something wrong with his clothing, but he wasn't wearing anything different to his normal work clothes. His dark trousers were a bit short, showing his white socks, but Flynn didn't think that was anything to get worked up about. His tweed jacket seemed clean enough, with no marks on it that he could see. He checked each elbow, and the leather patches were there as normal. Flynn shrugged. If it wasn't his clothes, it must be something else. He'd just had a haircut, so it was short, as regulations prescribed. He didn't have any tattoos, or deformities.

But Wright was speaking again, so Flynn listened closely.

'It seems you've crossed the line.'

Puzzled, Flynn looked down. 'I don't think so, sir, I can't see a line, can you?'

This time when Flynn looked back at his boss, there was a strange red flush all over his face. 'Are you alright, sir?' Flynn asked, afraid the man was about to suffer a heart attack or stroke.

'I will be very shortly,' Wright said. 'For you're being transferred.'

'Oh,' Flynn said, not know what to make of that. 'But I like it here in London, sir.'

'You might, but others don't. They find your, erm, shall we say, little ways, irritating and your complete disregard for procedure tantamount to mutiny.'

Flynn thought that last term very odd indeed, as he worked for the Metropolitan Police in London, not the Navy in Portsmouth, but the Chief carried on speaking before Flynn could correct him.

'We've decided to send you home, Flynn.'

'Home? Home where? Back to my flat?'

'No, home to Muddlebay. They need a detective there and as you know the area and the people it seems an ideal fit.'

'But I haven't been back for 10 years, sir, apart from the odd holiday.'

'No matter,' he said, brushing Flynn's protests away. 'Nothing much changes in towns like that. You'll keep your rank of Detective Sergeant but there isn't a team there. It'll just be you. The post calls for someone who works best alone and as I said, you seem the ideal choice. Think yourself lucky you're not being moved to traffic. I considered that, but you'd cause mayhem if the flow of traffic didn't work to your sense of order. Then I considered retraining as a dog handler, but of course you're allergic to dogs. My final thought was to give you the role of Desk Sergeant in reception. But you're so pedantic you'd never get anything done and the front reception would end up bulging at the seams. So home it is, to work alone, where you can't do any harm or fall out with your colleagues, as there won't be any.'

'But no one liked me in Muddlebay!' protested Flynn.

'No one is supposed to like a policeman, Flynn, so I'd say you've got a head start there!'

'But what if I don't want to go?'

'Listen,' Wright said, leaning over his desk, causing Flynn to take a step backwards. 'Do you want to remain a policeman?'

Flynn thought the question strange but answered truthfully, 'Of course, I do, sir.'

'Then take the posting. If you don't... let's just say you won't have a future in the police force. It's Muddlebay or nothing. Okay?'

Flynn managed to nod his agreement.

'Right, then, go and pack. You start on Monday, here are your orders.'

Flynn took the envelope the Chief held out, thanked him, and left his office, wondering what on earth was going on. But still, he only had a week to get organised, so he'd better make a start.

Chapter 2

Mabel Heggerty, Muddlebay Librarian, and font of all knowledge was in the children's section tidying up from the regular Wednesday morning story time. She pushed her white hair off her face and tucked it behind her ears. Her hair made her look older than she actually was, caused by the sudden death of her husband years before his time. A stalwart of Muddlebay, she'd lived there all her life and had never had any desire to move away. Why move to a larger place, where nobody knows you, nor cares about you? Although many had made the move, she had to acknowledge. As for her, she would be forever grateful to her many friends and acquaintances who had supported her in the dark days, weeks, and months after John's death. So she'd decided to stay in the community and give back to the town the best way she knew how, by ensuring they had a first-class library service on their doorstep.

The sun had come out after a short, sharp rain shower and Mabel stopped for a moment to savour the rainbow that had appeared in the sky. Then her interest was piqued by the sight of a man walking up the hill from the beach, towards the library. He had on a mustard-coloured tweed jacket and dark trousers with a red tie of all things. Clearly not a very colour co-ordinated individual. But there was something familiar about him, in the slope of his shoulders and his gangly limbs. As he raised his eyes from the pavement, she remembered who he was. Flynn Moran. As I live and breathe, thought Mabel, that was a name she hadn't heard in years. She had a vague recollection that he'd moved away to join the police force. His mother had continued to live in Muddlebay on her own, until her death, what, a year or so ago? As far as Mabel could recollect, the house was still empty, as though waiting like a desolate dog for an owner who would never return.

She remembered the first time she'd seen a young Flynn, running past the library as though a pack of wolves were on his heels. Which in a way they were. The local bully boys had obviously turned their attention to yet another victim, and the poor unfortunate was Flynn. The following day, the same thing happened. But on the third day, he'd skidded to a halt and ducked through the library doors. She could still remember him, stood before her with his ruffled hair, tie askew, blazer half off and a leather satchel with a strap sat cross ways over his body. Breathing heavily, he managed to gasp out that he'd like to join the library.

She smiled at the memory. From then onwards Flynn had come in most days. Sometimes to read quietly, on others to do his homework or research the topics being taught that term. He was a quiet studious boy who wore thick rimmed spectacles, making him look older than his tender years. He was uncoordinated, rubbish at all sports, but a whiz at puzzles. Mabel smiled and wondered what on earth he was doing back in Muddlebay. Wasn't he in London? She was sure she remembered an acquaintance telling her how proud Mrs Moran was of her son, a detective in the Metropolitan Police no less! That was one in the eye for all those who dismissed the boy as having no social skills and therefore no prospects.

As she put away the last few books, she glanced up at the wall, realising it was nearly lunch. Time to close the library for the day, being Wednesday half day closing. Perhaps she'd eat a sandwich down by the sea at her favourite spot on the pier, if it wasn't too windy. And so all further thoughts of Flynn Moran were driven away by hunger.

Chapter 3

Flynn had just had a nostalgic stroll by the sea, along the promenade, stretching his legs after the long journey from London. He'd even treated himself to a whippy ice cream, which brought back memories of his boyhood, the good ones, not the bad. He was pleased to find the ice cream still tasted the way he'd remembered it. Very few things did stay the same, he knew.

Plucking up his courage, he toiled up the hill to his old home. His mother's cottage, which was by rights, his cottage now. There being no other family members at the time of mother's death, he got the lot. A few thousand pounds and a cottage he didn't know what to do with.

Sell it? And have someone else trample over his memories? Not likely.

Holiday lets? Maybe, but they needed organising and that meant paying someone to do the cleaning and changeovers. Was it really worth it for the hassle and being taxed to death on the income? Probably not.

So in the end indecision had worked in his favour and meant he still had a home in Muddlebay. Flynn was grateful for small mercies.

He fished the keys out of his pocket. There was a key fob attached to the key ring, with the address on, as if he could forget it. He slotted the key into the lock and turned it, filled with trepidation. But instead of a musty, dusty, or even damp smell, his nostrils were assailed with the scent of furniture polish and bleach. Excellent. His solicitor had been as good as his word and arranged for someone to clean the cottage before Flynn arrived. It was bad enough having to face his memories, without being forced to face the fact that he'd neglected the property for so long.

The front door opened directly into a small living room, with a sofa and one armchair squeezed in, both facing an unlit fire and a television in the corner. He remembered how mum had liked her daytime telly programmes and smiled as he recollected some of the theme tunes. She was also a big soap fan, watching the three most popular programmes religiously every evening.

Walking through to the kitchen/diner he found everything gleaming. The fridge was turned on and opening it, he found that someone had left a carton of milk, one of orange juice, butter, and half a dozen eggs. There was fresh bread in the bread bin and a liner in the peddle bin.

Upstairs, the bed had been made in the main bedroom, his mother's old room. He wasn't sure about sleeping there, but let's face it the other bedroom only had a very small single bed in it and as he was now over 6', his legs would dangle over the end, so really, he had no choice. It wasn't as though his mother had died in her bed. She'd been in a hospice for the last few weeks of her life. The final room, the bathroom, was sparkling and as Flynn walked back down the stairs, he wondered what all the trepidation had been about. It wasn't so bad coming home after all. At least he had a sense of belonging in Muddlebay that he hadn't experienced in the huge and impersonal global city that was London.

He'd had to give notice on his lovely rented flat though, and he really must arrange movers. But first, he needed to go to his beloved Morris Minor 1000 Traveller, a classic British shooting brake car with a wooden frame and collect his suitcases from it. It was time to unpack.

Chapter 4

At 9am sharp on Monday morning, Flynn arrived at the Muddlebay police station, to find there was only two officers there, one of whom was sitting at the front desk. All was quiet. The other policeman was reading the paper with his feet up on his desk. Both were devoid of jackets and their shirt sleeves were rolled up, a far too casual look as far as Flynn was concerned and he clicked his tongue in disapproval.

Flynn introduced himself and produced his warrant card, saying that he was the new detective. The two men identified themselves as Sgt Fisher and Constable Elgin.

Looking around him, Flynn asked Fisher, 'Where are all the others?'

'What others?'

'The rest of the police officers, are they all out on a call? On the beat?'

Constable Elgin laughed so much that his feet slipped off his desk and he nearly fell out of his chair.

'I don't know if you've noticed, Detective Sergeant Moran, but this is a quiet place. In fact, you're the first detective we've ever had here.'

'Why?'

'Because nothing ever happens in Muddlebay,' and Fisher walked away still shaking his head and chuckling to himself.

It was left to Flynn to lift the counter and join

Fisher and Elgin in the small office behind it. Elgin pointed out Flynn's desk, placed in a corner as far away from Fisher and Elgin as possible in the small area. Flynn sat and looked around at his surroundings. The building was all dim and dingy, he decided. There was no buzz in the air. No ringing of telephones and clack of computer keys. No burble of conversation, nor any laughter. Just the ticking of a clock on the wall. It was all very depressing. Still he had to make the best of it.

'Are there any open cases I should be looking at?' Flynn looked over at the two men.

'No,' said Fisher.

Flynn opened every drawer in his desk. They were all empty apart from a bit of fluff in one and a red elastic band in another.

'Any old cases I can read through then?'

'Aren't any, sorry,' said Fisher.

'Why ever not?'

'Because nothing ever happens in Muddlebay,' the two men said in unison and sniggered. It seemed to Flynn they then deliberately turned their backs on him.

For want of anything better to do, Flynn decided to go for a walk around Muddlebay. He made sure that the two uniformed policemen had his mobile number in case of an emergency. What sort of emergency he didn't make clear. He only hoped Elgin and Fisher would, in time, take him seriously. In the meantime, he'd familiarise himself with his patch.

Outside, the weak sun was doing its best to peek

out from behind the threatening rain clouds and there was a brisk breeze blowing in off the sea. Flynn wished he'd put on his coat but wasn't going to go back and get it and give Fisher and Elgin something else to laugh at him for. Instead he buttoned up his jacket and stuck his hands in his trouser pockets.

Walking past the library, he was sure he heard someone call his name. He ignored it. The person called out again. He still ignored it. It was all rather disconcerting, as he quite liked the studied indifference people showed towards each other in London. Then a knock on a glass window brought him out of his reverie. He looked up to see a white-haired woman gesturing for him to go in. She looked vaguely familiar, but Flynn couldn't place anyone with white hair. Then it dawned on him. She must be the librarian, Mabel Heggerty. Glad to see a friendly face, he backed up the street and went in.

They went into the back office, where Mabel made them coffee and they quickly caught up on their respective lives over the past 10 years; Flynn being characteristically brief, not understanding why anyone would be interested in him. He learned from Mabel that her husband had died unexpectedly at a young age, hence her white hair, which had turned overnight. Flynn noticed she still wore the same style of clothes she had done for the past 20 years to his knowledge: a twinset, pearls and tweed skirt, accompanied by sensible shoes.

Mabel also told him that Muddlebay was getting

quieter and quieter. Less and less locals were able to afford the extortionate house prices being sought nowadays and that any available properties were being snatched up by out-of-towners for holiday homes.

'Oh dear, I was afraid of that,' Flynn said, but he couldn't help wondering what his cottage might be worth now. Turning to other things he said, 'There are two very under worked policemen at the station and they've told me nothing much happens here.'

'Oh, I wouldn't go so far as to say that,' said Mabel. 'Why don't you sit over there and read some back copies of the local weekly newspaper, to help you get a handle on what's happened since you left.'

At last, someone with a positive attitude, thought Flynn and settled himself down to work.

Chapter 5

Early the next morning, Flynn was woken by ringing. At first, he thought it was ringing in his ears, but then realised it was his much under-used mobile phone. He wasn't sure that anyone had his number, then with a start he sat up in bed and realised that no matter who it was, he really should answer it before it stopped ringing. He felt around for his mobile on the bedside cabinet, in the unfamiliar bedroom. Still befuddled from sleep, he managed to answer it without cutting the caller off.

'Moran,' he said hoarsely.

'Oh, Flynn, thank goodness you've answered. It's Mabel. The Mayor's wife, Jessie Carter, has found her husband dead in his chair. Looks like he never made it to bed last night. She slept through the night as she'd taken a sleeping tablet and has only just come across him.'

'How do you know?'

'Never mind that now, you should get over here. It's 1 West Villas,' and with that she was gone.

Flynn was glad she'd been suitably brief, as he couldn't abide unnecessary conversation and then leapt out of bed into the chilly bedroom. Grabbing his clothes, he jumped around the floor trying to get his trousers on, before stopping, telling himself more haste less speed. He must have looked like a Mr Bean figure rushing around and getting nowhere. So he stood still for a moment and then tried again.

He finally managed to get one limb in each trouser leg and rushed to the bathroom for a quick wash.

He was in his car when the next call came in. This time from Sgt Fisher.

'Ah, Moran, there you are,' the Sergeant said and proceeded to tell Flynn that the Mayor had been reported dead at home. 'I expect it's nothing more than a natural death, but I thought I'd let you know.'

It gave Flynn great satisfaction to tell Sgt Fisher that he was already on his way to the Mayor's residence, leaving the aforementioned policeman dumbstruck. Flynn disconnected the call with relish.

Flynn had no sooner pulled up outside 1 West Villas, when out of the front door came Mabel.

'What are you doing here?' he asked after he climbed out of his car. 'You can't be around a crime scene, you're a civilian.'

'Good morning to you as well, Flynn,' she admonished. 'Jessie Carter is my close friend,' she explained, 'so it was natural that I should come to her aid.'

Flynn supposed this was true. Not having much experience of friends, he decided that he better take Mabel's word for it.

'The ambulance has been called and I've notified Sgt Fisher,' she continued.

'Umm, well make sure you stay out of my way,' Flynn growled as he opened the boot of the car to retrieve his crime scene kit. Wondering if suiting up would be overkill, he settled for bootees for over his shoes and gloves. He gave a pair to Mabel. 'This might be a rather late precaution,' he told her, 'but I'd feel happier if you were at least wearing gloves and overshoes. Oh and don't let me forget to take your fingerprints for elimination purposes.'

'Oh, how exciting,' Mabel proclaimed, clapping her hands together. 'I've not had as much fun in ages.'

'Mabel, have some respect, a man is dead!'

'What? Oh yes, of course, sorry, Flynn. It's just that not much happens in Muddlebay.'

'So I've heard,' he said. 'Right, lead the way. And don't touch anything!'

At the front door both he and Mabel put on their bootees and gloves and Mabel led the way. Mayor Carter was in his study, sat in a large leather chair. Flynn prowled around the body. There was no disruption to the man's clothing, nor to the room in any way. Behind his wing-backed chair was a reading light positioned over his shoulder, which was still on. A book was open on his lap. With his head down and his eyes closed, it looked as though he had fallen asleep whilst reading.

'Where is Mrs Carter?'

'In the living room. She's very distressed, as you can imagine.'

'I'm sure she is, but I need a word with her.'

Mabel nodded and they turned from the body and walked through to the next room. Mrs Carter was a small, yet plump woman sat in a plump chair. She had rollers in her hair, with a hairnet over them, and a dressing gown was buttoned all the way up to her neck. In her hand was a screwed-up handkerchief and she was struggling to control her emotions.

'Mrs Carter?' Flynn asked.

When she nodded, he introduced himself and asked if she felt up to answering a few questions.

As she nodded her acceptance, Mabel slipped out of the room to make tea.

'Mrs Carter,' he began, taking a seat on the settee opposite her. 'Can you tell me what happened last night?'

'Nothing out of the ordinary,' she said. 'Alan came out of his study for dinner about 8pm and returned there around 10pm when I went to bed.'

'Did he leave the house at any point?'

She shook her head. 'No, he got in around 4pm that afternoon and had been indoors since then.'

'You didn't hear him moving about during the night?'

'No, nothing.'

'So he was just following his normal routine.'

Mrs Carter nodded as a fresh bout of tears burst forth. Luckily for Flynn, who never knew what to do in the face of emotion, Mabel returned at that point, and after putting down the tea tray, bent down to comfort her friend.

Flynn had just got his hands on a welcome cuppa, when the ambulance arrived. He reluctantly put down his cup and asked, 'Did the Mayor have any health issues?'

Mrs Carter nodded. 'Yes, a heart problem. He was on medication for it.'

'Thank you, where is it kept?'

'In the bathroom cabinet.'

'If you'll excuse me, I'll just go and get it and then see the paramedics.'

Chapter 6

As with all sudden deaths in England, there was to be a post-mortem. Flynn was very excited by this, but was careful not to show it. This was his world. He loved a good autopsy and in London had attended a surprisingly large number. Some wits had suggested that Flynn was the catalyst for the spike in deaths and when he left the Met, things would return to normal. Rather like an albatross foretelling death on a ship, the mere thought of DS Flynn Moran was enough to fell the ardent drug lord or burglar.

Ha ha, bloody ha, Flynn thought. Humour didn't have much of a place in his honest, down to earth world. He never really understood jokes. Was always the one looking puzzled at the punchline rather than rolling around belly laughing with the others.

But back to the matter in hand. Flynn had received a sideways look from the pathologist, Dr Stone, when he'd said he would be present at Mayor Carter's autopsy. But the doctor had, albeit reluctantly it seemed to Flynn, nodded his agreement. Hence Flynn was wearing a big smile and protective clothing and stood in the Autopsy Suite at the County Hospital. Familiar smells assailed his nostrils, able to get through the facemask without difficulty. The coppery smell of blood tinged with decomposition, overlaid with bleach, was a heady mixture of odours.

As he looked on, Flynn was quite taken by Dr Stone's glasses. They opened in the middle of the bridge for some unknown reason and hung around his neck on a cord, until needed. To Flynn it seemed an affectation, rather than something that was necessary or even useful. He wondered if the pathologist was the same in his dress, but, of course, for the moment Dr Stone was in scrubs.

As the pathologist worked and moved around the body, Flynn hovered behind him, tracking his movements, and looking over his shoulder.

'DS Moran, please stand still!' the exasperated pathologist said yet again. 'You're putting me off!'

'I'm just trying to get a better view,' grumbled Flynn. 'You keep getting in the way.'

'That's because I'm the pathologist and you are the policeman!'

Flynn wondered why the man had to keep insisting he knew what each other's roles were. To Flynn it was as plain as the nose on his face who held which job.

'Not that I know why you're here at all,' Dr Stone said.

'Because this is a sudden death and the Coroner requested an autopsy,' Flynn stated, wondering how such a man had managed all those years in medical school. It seemed his intellect was as thick as his middle.

'I know that, but it doesn't tell me why you are here,' said Stone turning on a bone saw.

Once the noise had died away, Flynn repeated,

'Because this is a sudden death, and the Coroner requested an autopsy.'

'But what has it to do with the police?'

Flynn noticed that Stone was going a strange puce colour. Maybe the stress was too much for the man. Flynn knew of several pathologists in London who had finally cracked under the strain of staring death in the face one too many times. Or maybe it was to do with the fact that, to be honest, the man looked as though he were morbidly obese, which couldn't be good for his blood pressure. But still, Flynn repeated patiently, 'Because this is a sudden death, and the Coroner requested an autopsy.'

Dr Stone closed his eyes and swayed on his feet, causing his assistant to ask if he was alright.

'I will be when this is over,' the man grumbled bad-temperedly and once more bent over the body, blocking Flynn's view, causing him to shuffle over so he could see.

And then it was over, and Dr Stone was stripping off his gloves.

'Well?' Flynn asked as he followed Dr Stone's lead and disposed of his protective clothing in the designated bin. 'What's the verdict?'

'Heart attack,' stated Stone.

'Is it that obvious?' Flynn wanted to know. 'Are you not waiting for toxicology?'

'Look, Sgt Moran,' Dr Stone stopped outside his office. 'Mayor Carter was an older male, overweight, with heart disease and taking medication. His was a death waiting to happen. Nothing more than that.

Now if you'll excuse me,' and Stone entered his office, slamming the door shut in Flynn's face.

Chapter 7

Once Dr Stone had sent in his autopsy report, the Coroner's Office released the body for burial. As the initial shock of her husband's death had worn off somewhat, Flynn wanted to interview Mrs Carter again. Mabel gently persuaded Flynn that she should be present as Flynn wanted to ask some rather stark questions about her husband's work, as he was wondering if the Mayor had had any enemies.

And so a date and time had been arranged and all three were at Mrs Carter's house. Flynn decided to get straight to the point, once the two women had been settled on a settee and Flynn in an armchair opposite them.

'Did your husband have any enemies?' was his entirely reasonable first question. At least entirely reasonable as far as he was concerned, but not to Mabel, nor to Mrs Carter.

It seemed Mabel was right in her assessment, as for some reason his question had brought on a bout of tears and Flynn had only been in the house a few minutes. He was beginning to think he didn't understand people in general and women in particular. Although, if he was honest with himself, that had always been the case, since his earliest memories at any rate.

'But the Coroner said he died of natural causes. Do you really think someone wanted to kill him?' Mrs Carter sobbed.

'Now, now, dear,' soothed Mabel, grasping her friend's hand and glaring at Flynn. 'That's not what Flynn meant at all, was it, Flynn?'

Having been briefed by Mabel beforehand, Flynn said, 'No, no, not at all,' although he kept his fingers crossed, hands hidden in his lap, as he'd just uttered a lie. And Flynn hated lies and lying, which was why he'd crossed his fingers, to negate said lie.

'There, see, dear?' Mabel said and this time she succeeded in stopping Mrs Carter's tears.

Flynn tried again. 'Had the Mayor been under any strain lately?'

Mabel nodded her approval of that question.

'He was always under some stress. Being Mayor of Muddlebay is quite a responsibility you know.'

'Exactly, that's why I asked.'

'Well, not so much being Mayor, that bit was rather nice,' explained Mrs Carter. 'We got to go to lots of civic events and I even had to buy some new hats.'

Fresh tears rolled down her face, which Flynn took as a bad sign.

But then she rallied. 'It was more stressful for him being leader of the council. He was a directly elected Mayor, you see, so he had mayoral and council roles.

'Now that is interesting,' said Flynn before he could stop himself.

'Why?' asked Mrs Carter.

'It's just that Flynn didn't know we'd changed electoral systems since he'd been away,' said Mabel quickly. 'Isn't that right, Flynn?'

'Yes, yes,' he said. 'That's all I meant, I'm very interested in local government,' and he got a smile of approval from Mabel for his quick thinking.

'I guess being Mayor, then, could have brought on a heart attack,' Mabel said. 'Especially as the poor man had heart disease that he was taking tablets for.'

Mrs Carter nodded, 'He'd put on a few pounds over the years and the hills around here didn't help, I suppose. But other than that... Honestly, he was very popular, wasn't he, Mabel?'

'Very, dear,' said Mabel stroking her friend's hand once again. 'Well loved by everyone I'd say.'

'Actually, Sgt Moran, I was wondering if you'd do me a favour, as you yourself hold a high office in our little community and I feel I can trust you. Would you be kind enough to gather up the Mayor's official papers for me from his study? Only the council need them back to pass onto his deputy and I just can't face them myself. Mabel said you'd be prepared to help me out and that I could trust you implicitly. Would that be alright? I'm afraid that they'll need sorting and collating, my husband wasn't the tidiest of people.'

Flynn couldn't help himself and a big grin split his face. That was just what he wanted, access to the Mayor's papers, and without having to ask! Perhaps there was something to be said for being a big fish in a small pond, instead of a small fish in the polluted sea that was London. It looked like people in Muddlebay might just be prepared to take him seriously, even though he was still having a few problems with Sgt Fisher and PC Elgin.

And who knew, he might even find a motive for murder without upsetting anyone! Yes, things were definitely looking up.

And so, just before Flynn and Mabel left Mrs Carter to her grief, he went into Mayor Carter's study once again. It seemed his wife wasn't exaggerating when she said her husband wasn't the tidiest of people. There were papers all over the desk and bulging out of two filing cabinets. It was clear Flynn would need more time to examine the contents. Leaving the study he arranged with Mrs Carter that he would return the following morning with boxes to collect the papers relating to official Muddlebay matters.

Chapter 8

A few days later, Flynn had just arrived home, the temping smells of a fish and chip supper making his stomach rumble, when the phone rang. It was Mabel.

'Mabel, I'm just about to eat, what is it?'

'This is no time to think about your stomach, Flynn, Mrs Carter has collapsed. She's unconscious in the chair at home. You need to get over here,' and Mabel cut the call.

Flynn looked longingly at his fish and chips, still in the wrapper from the chippy. Oh well, duty calls, he thought and grabbed his car keys. He arrived at Mayor Carter's house, just as his widow was being loaded into the ambulance.

'What on earth happened, Mabel? What were you two up to?'

'We had supper together, that's all. I've been keeping her company quite a lot lately. Anyway I was going to go into the kitchen to make the coffee when she decided to have a glass of port. So first of all, I went into the study and poured her a small glass and took it to her. I then went back into the kitchen. I'm afraid I was rather a while, as I decided to do the washing up while I was there, but she seemed happy enough. When I went back into the sitting room, she was having some sort of seizure, a fit, you know? She was shaking and unconscious, so I called an ambulance.'

'Did you have a glass of port?'

'No, I didn't.'

'Did the mayor drink port?'

'Yes, on occasion I suppose he did.'

'Come on,' said Flynn, 'we need to follow that ambulance.'

'But, Flynn, we know where it's going, to the County Hospital.'

'Oh, yes, right, let's get down there then.

'But what about my bicycle?'

'We'll come back for that later. This can't wait! I think Mrs Carter has been poisoned.'

Once at the hospital and upon ascertaining that Mrs Carter was in a cubical in A&E, Flynn used his warrant card and managed to speak to the doctor treating Mrs Carter.

'How is she, Dr Stride?' Flynn asked.

'Stable, at the moment. We're giving her fluids and monitoring her carefully. We're leaning towards a diagnosis of epilepsy.'

Flynn turned to Mabel, 'Has she ever had fits before?'

'Not that I know of,' answered Mabel. 'But I could be wrong.'

Turning back to Stride, Flynn said, 'Doctor, I think Mrs Carter may have been poisoned.'

'Poisoned? Whatever gave you that idea!'

It appeared to Flynn that Dr Stride was trying to hide his mirth at Flynn's outrageous suggestion. But Flynn wasn't having any of it and went on, 'Her husband died last month, unexpectedly and tonight Mrs Carter had a glass of the same port and collapsed. My friend Mabel here, didn't have any port and she's fine.'

'Really, Sgt, that's a bit random, don't you think? After all, nothing like that ever happens in Muddlebay.' The doctor put his hands in the pockets of the white coat he wore over scrubs and rocked backwards and forwards on his heels. His supercilious tone wasn't lost on Flynn, but after a scowl from Mabel Flynn managed to be civil. He said, 'Please, doctor, would you check for poison?'

'Which one, specifically?'

Stride's bored tone made Flynn want to arrest him on the spot, but he knew that being a pompous oaf wasn't exactly a criminal offence. Just an offence against Flynn's reputation as a detective. Even though the Doctor's tone was beginning to get on Flynn's nerves, he said politely, 'I'd say Deadly Nightshade.'

Flynn had to stand and silently witness the doctor breaking into gales of laughter. Determined to be heard, Flynn repeated his warnings, finishing with, 'Do you really want to be responsible for Mrs Carter's death if you don't act on my advice?'

That brought the man up short and perhaps gave him an inkling that Flynn could be right, or at the very least that he meant business. Mabel gasping at Flynn's words probably helped as well.

'Very well, I'll add your request to the blood screen,' and Dr Stride turned away, clearly still finding the whole conversation humorous, as his shoulders were shaking.

'What now, Flynn?' asked Mabel.

'Coffee while we wait and maybe a sandwich. My fish and chip supper is ruined now, and I haven't eaten.'

An hour later they were back in A&E. Flynn walked purposefully into the patient examination area casting around for Dr Stride.

'You go and see Mrs Carter, Mabel,' he said, 'I'll find the doctor.'

But the doctor found Flynn.

'How is Mrs Carter?' Flynn demanded. 'What were your findings?'

Dr Stride cleared his throat and seemed to have difficulty starting the conversation. 'Um, well, she has high levels of atropine in her system. Has she overdosed on her medication by mistake?'

'As far as I know she didn't take any! So she must have been poisoned then. I wonder who by?'

'That's your department, Detective. I just get her better,' and Dr Stride turned on his heel and walked away. No thank you, no well-done Flynn, nothing. Flynn shrugged. Let's face it he was used to it. People didn't like it when he was right and they were wrong, but there was nothing he could do about that. He turned and went to find Mabel and Mrs Carter.

Chapter 9

Finding Mabel still with Mrs Carter, he pulled her to one side and told her of the doctor's findings. 'So, Mrs Carter was the unwitting victim of her husband's poisoning,' Flynn concluded.

'From?' asked Mabel.

'Atropine, aka Deadly Nightshade. So, it was probably in the port. Come on, we need to rush back to the house,' Flynn said and dashed out of the door.

Mabel tried and failed to keep up with him and shouted after him, 'Flynn why are we rushing?'

Flynn stopped at the bank of lifts, allowing Mabel to catch up.

'Because that's what detectives do! Isn't it?' he asked, suddenly unsure.

'I'm finding all this rushing about exhausting.'

'Go home then,' said Flynn, not unreasonably.

'Not on your life,' said Mabel as the lift doors opened.

'Then stop moaning!'

'I'll stop moaning if you'll stop rushing,' Mabel countered.

As Flynn didn't want to continue investigating on his own, deciding he rather liked having Mabel with him to bounce ideas off, he had to agree. Thinking about it logically, he was half her age and therefore should be aware of her physical limitations. He figured that her local knowledge was proving to be invaluable, so he needed to accommodate her. He mumbled an apology of sorts and looked at the floor for the entire journey to the ground level.

Once at Mrs Carter's home, Mabel pulled the keys out of her handbag and they gained entry to the house, walking into the sitting room.

'First,' said Flynn as he pulled an evidence bag out of his pocket and snapped on gloves, 'where's the glass Mrs Carter drunk port from?'

Mabel pointed to it and Flynn put it carefully in the evidence bag, sealed it and wrote on the outside.

'Now, where's the bottle?'

'It'll still be in the study,' said Mabel and led the way, even though Flynn knew where to go. 'There,' she said, 'that's the bottle I used.'

Sat on a windowsill was a silver tray with a bottle of vintage port on it and one small port glass. Using his gloved hands, Flynn put the bottle in a further bag and then, for good measure, grabbed the other glass from the tray.

'Mabel?'

'Yes?'

'When the mayor died, had he been drinking?'

'Yes, I remember his wife saying he was given a bottle of port as a gift. She left him drinking it the night she went to bed early. Oh, that was the night he died!'

'Was this his glass?'

'Ah…'

'Aah what?'

'Well I tidied up and put everything in the dishwasher the next day. Still, I wasn't to know, was I? I was just helping out a friend.'

'Well, if the Mayor did have a drink and the port is laced with Deadly Nightshade as I suspect, he would have suffered a massive dose of atropine, as he was already on that medication for his dicky heart.'

Flynn started on a long-winded explanation of the effects of Deadly Nightshade on the body and how the sweet taste of it would have been masked by the sweetness of the port.

Mabel started rolling her eyes after five minutes, so Flynn guessed he better shut up and take her home. It was a shame, but some people clearly just didn't have the capacity for information that he had.

Chapter 10

It wasn't until a couple of days later that Mrs Carter was sufficiently recovered to leave hospital and go home and was also strong enough to talk to Flynn.

He wasted no time in asking, 'Who gave your husband this bottle of port?' and he showed her a photograph of it.

'Let me think,' she said.

Flynn hoped she wouldn't take too long thinking, as he was in rushing mode.

'Oh, one of his councillor friends, I think. Oh yes, the friend said he had a couple of bottles and thought the Mayor would like one of them.'

'Which councillor friend was that?'

'Um, I'm afraid I can't remember just now. It'll come to me I'm sure.'

'But...'

Flynn was cut short by Mabel raising her eyebrows at him.

'Could you ring me when you do remember?' he said, instead of urging the blasted woman to remember.

'Ah, so it's important is it?'

'Yes, very.'

'But it depends on the forensic testing of the liquid,' said Mabel. 'Doesn't it, Flynn?'

'Absolutely,' he agreed. 'But still, it would be very helpful to know who your husband got the port from.'

'I suppose I could check in his diary. That might ring a bell. Shall I do it now?'

'That would be very helpful, dear,' said Mabel. 'If you and Flynn go into the study, I'll make us a nice cup of coffee.'

The last thing Flynn wanted was a cup of coffee. He was eager to get the information and get on with the investigation. But if there was one thing he was learning from Mabel; it was that sometimes rushing and being so focused wasn't the best approach, even though it was normal for him. At least it had been when he was in London and dealing with the underbelly of society. He guessed things were a bit different in Muddlebay. Everyone seemed so much more relaxed and time seemed to move far slower than in the big city.

Flynn didn't necessarily like it, but he had to put up with it. His plan was to show everyone what a good detective he really was, so he would be able to return to the job he loved in London and to doing real detective work again.

Chapter 11

For once it didn't take long for the forensic tests to come back on the port and the pathologist rang Flynn with the results two days later.

'Good morning,' Dr Stone the pathologist, began. 'Well, we tested the bottle of port you brought in.'

'And?'

'And a foreign substance was found in it.'

'A foreign substance? Can you be more specific?'

'Atropine.'

'Deadly Nightshade,' breathed Flynn.

'Exactly.'

'In that case, how much would the Mayor needed to have drunk to kill him.'

'Oh, about half for that of a normal person.'

'Half?'

'Yes, I understand that the Mayor was already taking atropine for his heart condition, so drinking a couple of glasses of doctored port, well, it would be like him taking an overdose of his pills. Has it been known to happen before?'

'What?'

'Taking extra pills by mistake?'

'No and that certainly wasn't what happened. Not this time it wasn't,' said Flynn. Pausing for dramatic effect before saying, 'This time it was murder.'

'But,' spluttered the Pathologist. 'Nothing ever happens here in Muddlebay!'

Flynn smiled to himself as he replaced the telephone receiver. It seemed it was his job to prove that murder very definitely did happen in Muddlebay.

He mulled over the poison. Deadly Nightshade. Of course, the reason this one worked so well in the port was because the berries of Deadly Nightshade tasted sweet. Not that he tasted them personally. But he'd read that in a fermented drink, you probably wouldn't find much difference in the taste of say a red wine, port, sherry, mead, or ale. You would only be aware that there was a slight extra sweetness. It seemed Deadly Nightshade was the perfect poison for those who liked a tipple at the end of the day. But someone had put it in the bottle of port. Who? And Why Mayor Carter? Flynn would have to dig deeper and a good place to start was the library and Mabel.

Chapter 12

The same morning that Flynn got the report on the bottle of port that both Mayor Carter and his wife had drunk from, Mabel had a telephone call at the library from her friend, Mrs Carter.

'Mabel,' I've just remembered who gave the Mayor that bottle of port!' gushed Jessie.

'Oh, well done, dear.'

'Thank you. It had been bothering me, but after a good night's sleep I woke up with the name in my head.'

'Fancy that!' said Mabel.

'I know, spooky isn't it.'

'Yes, it is. So what is it, dear?'

'What's what?'

'The name of the person who gave the Mayor the port.'

'Oh yes, sorry, I was getting a bit distracted there. Well, it was Tom Ludlow. He's a Councillor and was a firm friend of the Mayor's.'

'Thank you, Jessie. I'll pass that information on to Flynn.'

'Oh, by the way, I wondered if you wanted to pop in for a sandwich for lunch, say 12.30?'

'That would be very kind, thank you. I'll see you then.'

Mabel replaced the receiver. Tom Ludlow, eh? That was a turn up. Tom was the last person that Mabel would have suspected to have done anything underhand, let alone try and poison the Mayor. It just didn't make sense. As she started on the big stack of books that needed returning to the shelves, Mabel turned the information over in her mind. She knew she'd have to give Flynn Tom Ludlow's name and also tell him of her concerns. The longer she pondered on it, the more she wondered if Mrs Carter had got the name right. She could quiz her more at lunchtime.

Surely it couldn't be Tom.

Could it?

Chapter 13

Mabel couldn't let Flynn know the name behind the gift of port straight away, as there were too many people in the library. For the next hour, Mabel had to content herself with returning books to the stacks. It was while she was in the cookery section that she became aware of a whispered conversation.

As she listened, she found the speaker was Tom Ludlow's wife no less, who was boasting in whispers to one of her cronies. She was saying that her husband could be made Mayor any day.

'But Mayor Carter's only just died!' her friend exclaimed. Mabel recognised the voice of Juliet Samson, an active member of the local Women's Institute and one of the women responsible for arranging the flowers in the local church.

'Yes, I realise that,' hissed Mrs Ludlow. 'But our little town needs a leader, don't you think?'

Mrs Samson murmured a reply that Mabel couldn't quite catch.'

'We wouldn't want anything getting out of hand. Tom would rule with a firm but fair grip.'

Mabel wasn't sure she liked the sound of that. It seems Mrs Ludlow was getting ideas above her station. Let's face it this was modern day Muddlebay, not George Orwell's 1984! Ruling with a firm but fair grip indeed. The very idea was preposterous. They didn't live in the time of Dickens, with a ruling class and an underclass.

Thankfully the two women left the library shortly after that, without either of them borrowing any books. As a result, Mabel wondered if it had been a secret tryst. But thought it probably hadn't been. It was pretty unlikely. The two were well known gossips and would have talked about the latest rumours over morning coffee, or even afternoon tea. On both occasions in public. So why the whispered conversation?

Deciding speculation was just wasting time, and as she had a break, she lifted the telephone and dialled Flynn's number.

Flynn was delighted with her call and wanted to go and see Tom Ludlow immediately. And for Mabel to go with him.

'But I have a lunch appointment in,' Mabel looked at her watch, '30 minutes. It will have to wait until the library closes.'

Flynn huffed down the line. 'But I wanted to go now.'

'Don't be petulant,' admonished Mabel, 'it doesn't suit you. An hour or two isn't going to make any difference.'

'It's longer than that,' said Flynn.

'And you can stop being so bloody pedantic as well, Flynn,' Mabel said, feeling that she was dealing with a surly teenager, not a seasoned detective. 'I've been invited to have a sandwich with Jessie Carter. She needs the company at this difficult time. I know how that feels and I won't let her down.'

'Oh, alright,' said Flynn, seemingly unable to

challenge that train of thought.

Perhaps just for once Flynn was showing some compassion, Mabel thought. After all the poor woman had just lost her husband and been poisoned herself. Although Mabel seriously wondered if Flynn would even recognise compassion if he saw it. She thought that to Flynn it was just some idealised state that people said he didn't have any of, and he'd no way of knowing how to get some. If something wasn't clear cut and black and white, he just didn't know how to deal with it.

'I'll meet you outside the library at 4.15 precisely,' he said to Mabel and he put down the phone, cutting off her call.

'Well, really,' said Mabel out loud.

'Problems, dear?' a woman asked in passing. It was one of Mabel's neighbours.

'Oh, no, just library stuff, you know.'

It was far more than that, but Mabel wasn't about to share her secrets with anyone. She made a point of listening to people whispering in her library, after all you never knew what they could be up to. But she never gossiped about it. But this time she might have to break her golden rule and tell Flynn about Mrs Ludlow's aspirations to be the next Lady Mayoress.

Chapter 14

At last it was 4.00pm and Mabel could close the library. By 4.10 she was locked up and waiting for Flynn outside on the pavement. With a hoot of his horn that told her he had arrived, he pulled over and swung open the passenger door for her.

'Right, where are we off to?'

'To see Tom Ludlow,' Mabel frowned, wondering what was wrong with Flynn.

'I know that, Mabel, but where does he live?'

'Oh, sorry, I see,' and she gave him the address.

On the way she told him about Mrs Ludlow's visit to the library, boasting how her husband was to be the new mayor.

'Do you think he will be?'

'More than likely. He's the best of a bad bunch if anything.'

Just then they pulled up outside an impressive Victorian villa.

'That looks worth a lot of money,' Flynn said.

'It does,' agreed Mabel.

'Conservative councillor, is he?'

Mabel laughed. 'Labour. He calls the house the fruits of his labour and says anyone can do what he has done with diligence and hard work.'

'A Tory by another name, then,' huffed Flynn as he climbed out of his car.

The man who opened the impressive black front door was of an equally impressive bulk. Mabel noted Tom had put on a lot of weight since she'd last seen him, what, about six months ago. Too much good living maybe? No doubt enjoying the fruits of his labours to the full.

Tom Ludlow seemed taken aback to see them on his doorsteps. 'Oh, hello, Mabel. Who's your friend?' he asked, looking askance at Flynn.

'Detective Sergeant Moran,' said Flynn waiving his ID under the man's nose. 'May we come in?'

Tom Ludlow shuffled backwards and invited them in with a nod of his head. Mabel and Flynn followed him through to a hallway with original black and white tiles on the floor and on into an impressive living room, complete with resplendent tiled fireplace.

'Nice place,' said Flynn.

'Thank you, but what can I do for you?'

Flynn ignored the question. 'Must have cost a pretty penny.' More a statement than a question.

'More like lots of elbow grease,' said Ludlow. 'But you still haven't told me why you're here.'

'We understanding you're running for Mayor,' said Flynn, staring at Tom Ludlow.

Mabel decided her friend was being deliberately antagonistic. Tom Ludlow must have thought so as well, for he didn't respond.

'Have you heard about Mrs Carter?'

'No, why?'

'She was poisoned with a bottle of port. As was her husband. And as you're in line to replace the Mayor, I wondered if you had any knowledge of that.'

It seemed Flynn wasn't about to pull his punches. Mabel stifled a grin.

'Of what?'

'Poisoned bottles of port. We're tracing them to their source. So how did you end up with one?'

Tom Ludlow sat down with a thump in an armchair. Flynn threw Mabel a smile and they sat on either end of a three-seater sofa.

'A bottle of port, you say?'

Flynn nodded.

'Like this?' and Ludlow sprang up and went to a dark wood cabinet that looked like a writing bureau. Pulling down the top of the bureau revealed an impressive array of bottles. 'For visitors,' Ludlow mumbled and pulled out a bottle of port. 'Is this what you're looking for?'

'Put it on the table please,' said Flynn, indicating the coffee table. 'Where did you get this?' Flynn asked.

'Someone gave it to me. In fact gave me two bottles. I knew the Mayor liked port, so I thought he'd like one of them. This one is mine.'

Flynn took an evidence bag out of his pocket and shook it open.

'You'll see I've not opened it.'

'Thank God for that,' breathed Mabel.

'I never had the occasion to drink it. In fact I'd forgotten it was there. Do you think that's doctored as well?'

'Forensic testing will tell us. In the meantime

please try and remember who gave you the two bottles of port. I'll be in touch.'

'Thanks, Tom,' Mabel said. 'We appreciate your help, don't we, Flynn?'

'Yes, yes, of course.'

Mabel thought Flynn sounded anything but thankful and threw Tom Ludlow a watery smile. She wondered if that was how the police normally conducted themselves. Flynn was acting as though Tom Ludlow was guilty of something. So once in the car, she decided to ask him.

'Do you suspect Tom of doctoring the port?' she asked as Flynn pulled into the passing traffic.

'I suspect everyone,' replied Flynn. 'I find that easiest.'

'But not Tom, surely? I can't see him doing anything like that. He's ambitious for sure, but plotting to kill Mayor Carter? I can't see it myself.'

'Let's just see what the lab says, shall we? Now, where do you want dropping off?'

That was clearly the end of the conversation, so Mabel asked to be dropped in the town centre as she had a bit of shopping to do.

As Flynn drove away from her, she couldn't help wondering whether Flynn's suspicions were founded in any sort of reality, or if he'd been reading too many detective stories. Or thinking he was still in London, seeing bad sorts on every street corner. The thought made her shudder.

Nothing much ever happened in Muddlebay and she desperately wanted it to stay that way.

Chapter 15

It was two days later when Flynn got a call from the forensic laboratory.

'Well, I don't know how you knew it, Flynn,' said Dr Stone. 'But you were right. The port had been doctored with Deadly Nightshade.'

'How did it get in there?' Flynn asked, 'because I couldn't see a break in the seal.'

'There was a small pin-hole in the side of the cap where a very fine syringe needle had been put into it. We would have missed it if you hadn't asked us to carefully check for one.'

'That's great, Doctor. Thank you.'

Flynn replaced the receiver and sat and looked at it while he thought.

'What you up to, Met?' asked Sgt Fisher. 'You're staring into space. Using those little grey cells, are you?'

Flynn was getting very fed up with the teasing from Fisher and Elgin. He hoped the novelty would wear off sooner rather than later. They'd taken to calling him 'Met' as he used to be in the Metropolitan Police. But not content with that, also kept making references to Poirot, Sherlock Holmes and any other fictional detective that came to mind.

Flynn ignored their scrutiny and pondered his knotty problem. Was someone trying to kill Tom Ludlow as well as the Mayor? Or were both bottles doctored as the killer couldn't guarantee that the right bottle would go to the right victim. A fifty-fifty chance of the plan coming to fruition wouldn't be good enough odds. If they intended to kill the Mayor, or Tom Ludlow, they had to be sure it would happen and have a reason for doing it. Which led him to try and imagine what that reason could possibly be. He needed to do more investigation. Looking at his watch he saw it was past 10 am so the library would be open. He needed to talk to Mabel and then see Tom Ludlow again. For the man could be in danger. He really didn't think that Ludlow was the killer, for surely he wouldn't be so stupid as to leave another bottle of doctored port in his own house, where anyone could access it. If Ludlow had known it was poisoned, surely, he would have disposed or it, or even kept it in a locked safe, where it couldn't inadvertently do any harm.

Mabel wasn't at the library when he arrived, which threw Flynn. Luckily, her colleague told him that it was Mabel's day off and she'd be at home, apparently doing some Spring cleaning. As Flynn emerged from the library straight into a rain shower and a blustery wind that threatened to blow his umbrella inside out, he wondered about the term, 'Spring cleaning'. It certainly wasn't Spring yet, being February. He shook his head. There were just some things that didn't make one iota of sense to him.

Luckily, he did find Mabel at home, resplendent in yellow rubber gloves, pink apron, and green headscarf. Even if the time of year wasn't right, her clothing was, if rather garish. When he told her of his findings and thoughts, it took but a minute for her to disrobe and grab her handbag.

Looking at the weather, Mabel said she thought Ludlow would be at home. He wouldn't be at the Council offices as there were no meetings that day and the weather was too bad for him to be out and about in the area doing whatever it was that he did, like playing golf on the local course, more often than not.

Flynn was relieved to find Ludlow at home. To be honest he hadn't fancied driving around the area in the awful weather, tracking the man down. Flynn and Mabel left the car and were blown to Tom Ludlow's front door by a particularly vicious gust of wind.

Once they'd gained entry, Flynn told Tom Ludlow that his bottle of port had also been doctored with Deadly Nightshade.

Ludlow sat down in his chair with a thump and all the colour drained from his face.

'Would anyone want to kill you?' Flynn asked and got a kick in the ankle from Mabel. Presumably because she thought he was being too direct. Again. Still, he was a policeman – no, a detective - and he didn't have time to mess about with niceties. Anyway he wasn't much good at them. But looking at Tom Ludlow, Flynn saw the man had turned grey and Flynn was afraid Tom was going to have a heart attack.

'Bloody hell, not that I know of,' Ludlow managed to gasp.

'Can you remember who gave the bottles to you?'

'Well, I don't like to say...'

'I'm afraid you must say. Otherwise I shall arrest you for perverting the course of justice.'

Mabel gasped. 'Flynn you wouldn't!'

'I jolly well would, Mabel. So, Mr Ludlow, which is it to be? Are you going to give me the information I require? Or go to the police station in handcuffs?'

That drew another gasp from Mabel.

'Oh, alright then,' said Ludlow belligerently. 'They were a gift from a property developer. Councillors are not supposed to take any gifts, as they could be construed as bribes. That's why I didn't want to tell you. I'm not going to get into trouble, am I? Oh, God, I could be an accessory after the fact! Will I go to prison?'

'Let me see if your story checks out first. Which developer was it?'

'It was Blacknote Developments, but they were sent via their builder. Prior's his name. Oh, God, what will this do to my chances do you think?' and Tom ran his hand over his face.

'Chances?'

'Yes, I'm running for Mayor, as you probably know.'

Flynn ignored Ludlow's moaning. 'So you were given two bottles of port by Blacknote Developments. And what else?'

Ludlow's mouth opened and closed like a fish,

but eventually he said, 'When I was given them, I said I didn't much like port, but thank you anyway. So it was suggested that as the Mayor liked the stuff why not give them to him? You're lucky I remembered. We get lots of stuff like that around Christmas you know.'

With that Mabel and Flynn left Tom Ludlow chewing the side of his mouth and looking very worried indeed.

As Flynn was preparing to drive away, through his rear-view mirror he saw Tom Ludlow leaving his house and hurrying to his car. He looked like a troubled man and Flynn said as much to Mabel, adding, 'Well, well, fancy Tom Ludlow, local councillor, in the pocket of a developer. I reckon he's off to see Blacknote Developments.'

'He's definitely bothered, but who wouldn't be?' said Mabel looking in the wing mirror at the man scurrying to his car.

'He's either bothered, or guilty,' countered Flynn.

'Guilty of what?'

'Trying, and succeeding, to kill Mayor Carter.'

Mabel gasped again.

As Flynn drove back to town he pondered if Tom Ludlow could really be the killer.

Did he want high office in Muddlebay?

And was he prepared to do whatever it took to get it?

Chapter 16

'Mabel,' said Flynn as they drove back into Muddlebay town centre, 'do you know this developer chap Black? Is he just a builder? Or does he own any land himself?'

'I think he owns the land and the man called Prior that Tom told us about, builds whatever on it for him.'

'Hmm, interesting. Can you get me a list of the planning applications before the council at the moment, and any recent ones that have been rejected?'

'Of course, I'll get the information for you first thing tomorrow morning.'

'Tomorrow? What's wrong with now?'

'It's my day off, Flynn, or have you forgotten?'

Flynn clearly had. 'But, Mabel,' he countered. 'This is really important. There'll be other days off.'

'Oh very well,' she agreed after a short pause, 'the library it is.'

When they arrived, Mabel insisted Flynn get them cups of coffee from her favourite café while she gathered the information he wanted. By the time he got back, he had two large coffees and she had a stack of applications on the conference table in the back office.

There were a surprising number, Flynn decided. Although to be fair most were for extensions, or garden buildings, Muddlebay being in a conservation area and on the edge of the Green Belt. Both of which severely restricted the amount and type of developments that would be approved by the Council.

'So,' Flynn said as he sat down. 'What type of building does this Blacknote Developments do?'

'Oh, I'd say new houses every time. And thanks for the coffee.' Mabel toasted Flynn with her cup and took a satisfying gulp of it.

Flynn ignored his own as he poured over the proposed new developments.

'What about this one? It's an application by Blacknote Developments for six houses on the edge of the green belt. That looks like a good fit. Right, I'm off to the planning department to get the full details. I'll be back in a bit.'

'Not here you won't be. I'm off home, in fact you can drive me back there. If you want to talk about your findings, pop back to the house.'

Flynn thought Mabel was pushing her luck, after all he had just bought her a takeaway coffee. Still, he didn't want to alienate her, she was the only person in Muddlebay who had time for him. Let's face it he wasn't one for gossiping over the garden fence with the neighbours, and anyway people always wanted to talk about the latest crime and Flynn absolutely refused to discuss an open investigation. Unless it was with Mabel, of course.

By the time he'd dropped Mabel off, driven to the Council offices and parked the car, it was lunchtime when he arrived at the door to the Planning Office. To find it closed for lunch. No amount of rattling of the doorknob or rapping on the wood raised anyone, which frustrated Flynn beyond belief. He stormed back down to reception, determined to take someone to task. But there was no one there either. It seemed the whole building shut for lunch! Preposterous! But there was nothing to be done about it, so Flynn went back to his car and sat there, going over his notes on the investigation and testing out theories.

On the stroke of 2pm he was waiting outside the Planning Office when a man ambled up brandishing a set of keys tied to his belt on a long chain, reminiscent of a prison warder. He unlocked the door and Flynn was hot on his heels, following him into the room before the man could object. Flynn held up his warrant card and demanded full details on the latest planning application by Blacknote Developments.

'When for?' the man asked, licking a pencil, and grabbing a notebook.

'Now.' Flynn folded his arms, determined not to leave without the information.

'Now? I'm afraid that's not how it works. You have to fill in a requisition form with the complete details, reference number etc and I could have them for you in a couple of days. That do you?'

'Absolutely not,' said Flynn. 'I need them now.'

'But I've just told you…'

The man didn't get any more words out as Flynn held his ID in the man's face. 'I'm investigating a murder. I need that information NOW otherwise there could be serious consequences.'

'M, m, murder? C, c, consequences?'

All of a sudden, the clerk was reduced to jelly, which Flynn, if he was honest, found very satisfying. It was about time he was more forceful, he decided, if the man's reaction was anything to go by.

'That's what I said. Now are you going to help me, or must I go to your boss, or your bosses' boss, or whoever is in charge of the whole damn building and tell them what a piss poor job you're doing and that, furthermore, you were deliberately trying to derail a murder investigation.'

Flynn stopped gabbling but was rather proud of his forthright behaviour. It was clearly about time he grabbed Muddlebay by the scuff of its neck and shook it until the clues dropped out. Or some such. 'Now hurry up,' he growled as the man scurried away.

To be honest Flynn's display of bravado owed much to detective television programmes made in the 1970's such as The Sweeney, and the more recent Life on Mars which was set in the 70's. It wasn't like Flynn at all. Very out of character. But at the same time it had been rather fun and Flynn saw that it had worked a treat, as the clerk came through from the back office with files, maps and drawings clasped in his arms.

'Here's a full set of the plans, the application and details of the landowner and the architect.' He dumped them on the counter and Flynn promptly scooped them up.

As Flynn left, the man called after him, 'Would

you put in a good word with the Chief Constable for me? I wouldn't mind a round of golf with him one day. Battles is the name!'

Chapter 17

Flynn went straight to Mabel's house, cleared her dining room table, and laid all the stuff from the planning office on it. Mabel came from the kitchen with two teacups in hand to find Flynn had taken over her table and was just about to tape stuff to the glass on her patio doors.

'Flynn!' she barked. 'Stop it! I've just cleaned those.'

Flynn huffed, but placed the documents back on the table and rubbed at the offending marks with the sleeve of his tweed jacket, which to be honest just made the smudges worse. At a black look from Mabel he remembered to thank her for the cup of tea and invited her to join him looking over the plans.

'Right, so what have you got here, Flynn?' said Mabel, appearing slightly mollified.

'There's a proposed development on the edge of town for six new dwellings, with the land purchased by Blacknote Developments from the owners of six houses. He plans to build on their back gardens, one dwelling on each plot.'

'What sort of dwellings?'

'Well originally they were five bedroomed detached houses.'

'Originally?' asked Mabel.

'Yes, but that scheme got turned down, deemed as too high density for the area.'

'And now?'

'Now Blacknote want to build six three-bed-roomed bungalows, all high spec, each sitting in approximately quarter of an acre. He's also proposing to build a new access road, so the bungalows face away from the houses and the two back gardens meet.'

'That sounds better. Less obtrusive. But very expensive. Anybody would think we lived on Sand-banks,' said Mabel with a snort of derision. 'This is Muddlebay for goodness sake. If you ask me, some people, such as Black, have ideas above their station.'

'It's called gentrifying, Mabel.'

'Well I wish they'd leave us well alone. We don't need any of that nonsense here.'

'You need to move with the times.'

'No I don't and that's all there is to it. Nothing ever happens in Muddlebay and that's just the way we like it,' a disgruntled Mabel folded her arms across her chest. 'When's the hearing?'

'That's the thing, Mabel, it's in two night's time.'

Chapter 18

'Right then,' said Mabel and grabbed her coat. 'We best be off!'

'Where to?'

'The building plot, of course.'

'Do you know where it is?'

'I was born and bred here, Flynn, of course I do, and anyway there's not much that gets past me.'

As they battled the rush hour traffic across town, Mabel told him what she'd heard about the proposed development.

'It was a couple of years ago now, when Joan Simms was telling her friend about her windfall as they browsed in the craft section. I was in the next stack along. I couldn't see who Joan was talking to, so I pulled out a couple of books and peered through the crack. I realised it was one of her neighbours, Conny Stephenson. Anyway, Joan was saying that she'd been approached by Black asking if he could buy half her back garden and he offered her £25,000. Now, I happened to know that Joan needed the money as her husband had recently died and she didn't want to have to sell her lovely family home, but would have had problems with the upkeep on just her pensions. So, she was doing her best to convince Conny to talk to Black herself.'

As Mabel drew breath, Flynn jumped in. 'So he needed all six plots?'

'Yes. Apparently, he wouldn't buy Joan's unless

the other five homeowners would sell as well. She was telling Conny that there was no way Black would get planning permission, as they lived on the edge of the green belt, so it was a win-win for the six homeowners. A cash windfall and only half the garden to have to mow. What was not to like?'

'And Conny fell for it?'

'Oh yes, and between them, Joan and Conny persuaded the other four to sell as well and so Black had his land at a knock down price as there was no planning permission at that stage.'

'Do you know why it was turned down the first time?'

'Well,' said Mabel clearly about to launch into another long-winded gossipy tale, much to Flynn's horror. 'I heard from Mrs Carter that it was the Mayor who had put the kibosh on the first scheme. He'd persuaded one of the other councillors to vote with him as well, against the plan.'

'Do you remember who that was?'

Mabel clasped her hand to her mouth. 'Oh gosh! It was Tom Ludlow!'

Flynn decided to tackle that tasty morsel later, as they'd just arrived at the building plot. There was nothing there apart from a huge board saying that coming soon was a development of six luxury houses and to contact Blacknote Developments to register interest. With a large-scale drawing in hand, Flynn and Mabel walked around the land identifying where the six bungalows would go. Until Mabel stopped so suddenly that Flynn crashed into her.

'Look, Flynn, here it is, Deadly Nightshade!' She was pointing to a plant. Then she scrabbled in her handbag. 'I took a photocopy of a picture of the plant from another book on poisons we had in the library. Look, here, the plant is identical to the picture.'

'Wait. You've got two books?'

'Well, yes. Slightly different from the other one but it covers a lot of the same ground.'

'Can you tell me who took that one out?'

'Of course, we have the borrowing history stored on the computer.'

Flynn looked at his watch. It was 6pm so nothing much else could be done that night as the library had automatic time locks on it and the authorities would be called if Mabel tried to get in now. Even though Flynn was police, he couldn't just enter any premises he felt he needed to whenever he wanted, much to his frustration.

'I need to see that book and the borrowing history, Mabel. I'll come to the library first thing tomorrow morning and we can go through it.'

Chapter 19

The next day, after calling into the police station and finding that no one had missed him, nor cared if he was there or not, Flynn went to the library to meet Mabel.

'Ah, there you are, Flynn,' Mabel called.

There were a number of browsers in the library and all of them turned and inspected Flynn as though he were a member of an unknown species, who had landed in Muddlebay from a faraway galaxy. There was the dour spinster type, who frowned at him over her glasses. The country gent who harrumphed at the disruption and the young mother who scowled at him for distracting the infant she was reading to in the kiddie's corner.

'Come through to the back,' Mabel suggested in a whisper, and he gratefully accepted her suggestion.

Once there, Mabel handed him several sheets of paper.

'What's all this?'

'The information you wanted on people borrowing the books about plants and poisons, of course.'

'But there's loads of books and loads of borrowers!'

'I know that Flynn I compiled the list,' said Mabel rolling her eyes. 'The information on deadly plants or deadly poisons crops up in more than two books you know. So I made sure I included all books that had references to poisonous plants in them.'

'No, I didn't know that, or realise that, or re-member that.' Flynn realised he was going down a rabbit hole and shut up. 'Well, I'll need some help going through these names,' he muttered under his breath.

'Oh for goodness sake, stop moaning. Anyway there's a lot of red herrings in there I imagine,' said Mabel.

'Red herrings?'

'Yes, people who have absolutely nothing to do with our case, but their names are on the list and are muddying the waters.'

'Muddying the waters? What waters? The sea?'

'Flynn, are you for real today? Did you miss breakfast? Or your morning coffee? They're just say-ings. Idioms. Don't you ever use… no I don't suppose you do. You're too literal for that.'

But Flynn wasn't listening to Mabel's prattling any longer, he was far more focused on finding their killer, than having a discussions about old fash-ioned sayings, that he didn't understand. In fact had never understood. So he sat down, got a pen out of his pocket, and pulled the papers towards him.

After an hour or so of crossing out names, books and other sundry items, Flynn came across some-thing of interest.

'Look at this,' Flynn said to Mabel as she walked back into the room and he handed her a piece of paper. It logged an entry showing that Judith Black took out a book on poisons, itemised in her borrow-ing history.

'Didn't you notice when she passed the book to you for checking out? I thought that with everything that's been going on you would have recalled such a transaction.'

'No, everything is automated now, Flynn.'

'Really?'

'That just shows how long it's been since you borrowed anything from a library,' smiled Mabel. 'Members return and take out their own books, using the machines. Anyway, when you said you wanted details of who had borrowed a book on plants, I included the borrowing history of anyone who seemed suspicious or related to the case in some way. And that's how I found Judith Black.'

'Mabel you're a genius. We'll make a detective out of you yet!'

'Oh, Flynn,' Mabel said as her eyes suddenly became moist. 'That's the nicest thing anyone has said to me for a long while. You know, I'm awfully glad you returned to Muddlebay.'

Chapter 20

'Are we going to arrest Judith Black now?' Mabel said as she pulled her coat on.

'Not just yet,' said Flynn. 'We can't arrest anyone on their borrowing history without any other corroborating evidence.'

'Oh,' Mabel appeared deflated. 'I was looking forward to a bit of excitement. You know, flashing lights, sirens, handcuffs...'

Flynn shook his head and wondered how he was ever going to survive being a detective in Muddlebay. It wasn't that Mabel didn't take him seriously, more that she watched too many police series on the television.

'We're off to see Ian Prior.'

'Really?'

Flynn sighed. 'Yes, really, Mabel. Why would I tell you lies?'

'I didn't mean any such thing as you well know,' she admonished.

'Mabel, get in the car please, otherwise we'll spend your entire lunch hour bickering.'

At last Mabel did as she was told and Flynn drove them to the outskirts of town where Ian Prior had an office on a small industrial park, next to a rather large and noisy builder's merchants.

As they walked in, Flynn took out his identification and asked the young woman if they could speak to Ian Prior.

'No sorry, dad's having his appendix out today.'

'And you are?'

'Hello, Chrissie,' said Mabel. 'How are you?'

'Oh, hi, Mrs Heggarty. Alright, you know. It's just, like, with dad being off for the next few days, it's pretty quiet around here. Still, I'm able to get my nails done. What do you think?' and she waived her hand under Mabel's nose.

Before Mabel could reply, Flynn intervened, cutting short any conversations about nails. 'We're here about bottles of port.'

'Eh? Sorry you've got the wrong place. Maybe you want the cash and carry next door?' she grinned. 'Bottles of port! That's a good one, innit?'

Flynn swallowed down his irritation. Couldn't the girl take anything seriously? To Flynn she looked the epitome of a dizzy blond. Her hair was thick and coiled and held off her face with slides. She had poked pencils in it to look like chop sticks and her clothing was an eclectic mix of colours and styles. She had bright red lipstick on to match her blood red nails.

'Who are you?' he barked.

Mabel shot him a look and said, 'This is Chrissie Prior, Ian's girl. Chrissie this is Detective Sgt Flynn.'

'Police?'

Chrissie had paled at the information.

'Yes, why?' asked Flynn.

'Well, if it's about the illegal rave the other night, I had nothing to do with it, honest.'

Flynn had no idea what she was talking about.

'We're here about any gifts of port that your father may have been given,' he said.

'Oh, those, well why didn't you say so before? I remember those, they stayed in the office for, like, ages. They were up on that shelf there, two of them. Then all of a sudden, they were gone. I asked dad about them and he said he'd no idea what I was talking about. He'd didn't remember seeing any port and hadn't given anyone any either. That was all. I don't know anything else.'

'You don't know where he got them from?'

'Like I just said, I don't know anything else about them. Look, we get a lot of stuff like that around Christmas, you know. People are always doling out lots of booze. I normally pinch them when dad's not looking, but I don't like port, so I left them alone.'

'When did you notice they'd gone, dear?' asked Mabel.

'Hmm,' Chrissie scratched her head with a long red fingernail. 'Sorry Mrs Heggarty, I can't remember.'

Fynn thought that Chrissie had probably had a close shave with death, but for once decided he'd best keep that nugget of information to himself. As they left, Flynn noticed Chrissie Prior lift her mobile phone to make a call and begin chewing on the end of her pencil, as if chewing over a particularly knotty problem. He wondered who she was calling and what secrets she hadn't shared. He wasn't altogether taken in by the dizzy blond persona.

Chapter 21

As he and Mabel drove away, Flynn ruminated on their current conundrum. 'So, we have the builder, Ian Prior, in hospital with appendicitis, who may have given the Mayor the doctored port, via Tom Ludlow.'

'Do you think Prior is in danger?'

'Prior? Why do you think that, Mabel?'

'Because if Prior knows the port was doctored, the killer could decide that the builder knows too much and try and get rid of him! Or perhaps one of the bottles was meant for Prior himself and the killer is wondering why Prior's not dead!'

'Mabel, you have a very devious mind!'

'Flynn, when you've seen the things I have in my 60 odd years, then you'd have a suspicious mind as well.'

'Hang on, how will Prior know the port was doctored?'

'You saw Chrissie pick up the phone as we were leaving. My guess is that she was calling her dad to let him know we've been to the office and what we wanted. I don't think for a minute she's as stupid as she appears to be. Or would like people to think she is. She was very bright at school you know, passed her exams with flying colours.'

Flynn noted Mabel's idiom 'flying colours' and wondered how many more Mabel had in her store of useless sayings. Still, he appreciated her help and her company, it was turning out to be not such a bad posting after all, Muddlebay, for he'd not had as much fun in ages!

After dropping Mabel back at the library, Flynn reluctantly returned to the police station, where he would have to face Fisher and Elgin. Luckily only Fisher appeared to be around, and Flynn managed to make it to his desk without the man taking the micky out of him. Once there, he pulled a clean piece of paper out of his drawer and began to jot down his thoughts and findings.

The Builder: Ian Prior, wife Connie Prior, daughter Chrissie Prior and son Cameron. He had bottles of port on the shelf that have since gone. Both to Tom Ludlow.

The developer: John Black and Judith Black owners of Blacknote Developments and their son Ollie. Who gave the port to Prior?

Tom Ludlow: councillor in the pocket of developer. Given two bottles of port and it was suggested that as the mayor liked the stuff to give them to him.

Mayor Carter who died from drinking the port. His wife Jessie who was also poisoned and taken to hospital and survived.

He drew lines, bubbles, and Venn diagrams, as he thought through various theories and either kept them or tossed them. Finally, the pieces of the puzzle fell into place and Flynn had hatched a plan, the execution of which would call for perfect timing. He was sure Mabel would help him. She had to, as she was a vital piece in the puzzle. He reached for his phone and called her.

In response to his call for help, she said, 'Of course, Flynn, just tell me what you want me to do...'

Chapter 22

Flynn was deep in thought as he drove to inter-view the owner of Blacknote developments. He approached the house, discreetly nestling in a country lane surrounded by other large, well maintained properties, pondering at the wealth on show. Manicured lawns and pristine gravel were the first impressions, followed by gardens that looked like they'd been designed and executed by Charlie Dimmock. He guessed that if you develop luxury houses, then you'd better have a luxurious house yourself. And then keep it. The climb down from such a high social standing would be embarrassing in the extreme. Is that what kept Black going? His social standing within the community? Who knew? But there was definitely something rotten happening in Muddlebay and it was Flynn's job to find out who was causing it and cut out the rotten part of the town.

He slowed down to pass a woman walking her very muddy dog, who was carrying a large stick in its mouth. She blended into her surroundings, wearing green and brown clothing, and had wellingtons on her feet that Flynn was pretty sure were Hunters. Yes, the Black family had done rather well for themselves.

Flynn crunched over their drive and pulled up outside the house, parking in the generous turning circle. There was a triple garage, with the doors open, housing two luxury cars and a motor bike. An ear-splitting creak heralded his arrival as he opened the door of his old Morris Minor and climbed out.

The front door opened, and John Black was standing there. It was time to take him to task over the murder of Mayor Carter.

Mabel climbed off the bus, glad the rattling journey was over. She decided she was getting too old for public transport. The problem was she didn't have a car and that buses were free due to her bus pass. So she was pretty sure she'd have to keep riding them if she wanted to go anywhere.

Clutching her handbag and a paper bag of grapes, she made her way into the hospital. Enquiring at the reception desk where her friend was located, she rode up the three floors in the lift to a surgical ward. Spying the family in the last bay on the right, she smiled her way down the ward towards them.

Chapter 23

John Black didn't seem at all pleased to find Flynn on his doorstep, he pursed his lips and said, 'How can I help you, Sgt Flynn?' managing to sound as though Flynn was something dirty on the bottom of his shoe.

Flynn ignored the jibe. He'd been called too many names by hardened London criminals, and so obnoxious people like Black didn't bother him. 'I need to speak to you about the death of Mayor Carter, Mr Black.' Flynn noticed a neighbour stood at the end of the drive looking rather interested in Mr Black's visitor. 'I think indoors would be best, don't you?'

'Oh very well, although I don't know what this has got to do with me,' said Black and turned on his heel.

Flynn closed the door behind himself and then followed Black into a contemporary living room. Mrs Black was sat on one of the settees and John sat next to her, although Flynn noticed that they didn't touch.

'As you know, Mayor Carter has been murdered,' he began, 'and Mrs Carter only just survived being poisoned as well. Deadly Nightshade was in the bottle of port that they had both drunk from.'

'Well, that's very sad and all, but what the hell has it got to do with us?'

'I have reason to believe the gift of a bottle of

port had originally come from Blacknote Developments.'

Black spluttered and said, 'You can't be serious, surely? I don't know anything about it. I am denying all knowledge of port or poisons. The whole idea is bloody ridiculous!'

Mrs Black said nothing, but she had gone very pale.

'Here's the way I see it,' said Flynn. 'Ian Prior is in hospital having his appendix out, but he has been helping me with my enquiries. Mr Prior had two bottles of port in his office. They were a gift and had been left on a shelf for quite some time and forgotten about, before being passed on. These bottles of port had been doctored with Deadly Nightshade. When Prior comes round from his operation, I am sure he will be able to name the person who gave him the bottles of port and told him to pass them onto the unsuspecting Mayor.'

'Really, Sgt Flynn,' said Judith Black. 'What has any of this got to do with us? Why on earth are we of interest in this case?'

'Because Blacknote Developments are trying to get planning permission for six houses,' said Flynn, being as patient as possible, although their denials were grating on him and he wished Mabel were with him. But that would have foiled their plan, so Flynn knew he'd better try his hardest to appear normal. Whatever normal was.

'When Blacknote Developments wanted to build six luxury houses on plots purchased from homeowners who were willing to sell part of their back gardens, the Planning Committee were split on the proposal and in deadlock, so Mayor Carter had the deciding vote and turned the proposed development down. You have since revised the plans to build six luxury bungalows instead of houses and the resubmitted plans will be voted on tonight.'

'Are you really saying that we'd want to get rid of Mayor Carter because he's against any development in that part of Muddlebay? The idea is preposterous.'

'That's exactly what I'm saying, Mr Black. But there's one other piece of the puzzle that I haven't told you about yet.'

Both Mr and Mrs Black leaned towards Flynn, seemingly keen to hear his final piece of evidence. 'I know Mrs Black borrowed a book on poisons from the library,' he finished with a flourish.

'You must be mad! Why would I do that? Why would I want to kill anyone?' Judith Black cried, looking from her husband to Flynn and back. 'John? What is he talking about? I don't understand!' she said and started crying.

Flynn was very pleased to have provoked a reaction from Judith Black, as well as from her husband, who was on his feet and looming over Flynn. However, Flynn wasn't about to be intimidated by a suspect and continued with his interview.

'I've been wondering why you did it, Mrs Black? Why you tried your hardest to help get the planning permission? Is it because you like the money the company brings in? You didn't want the flow of cash to dry up? You enjoy your shopping trips too much, don't you?'

'Now I really think you're mad,' she retorted, drying her tears. 'We're upstanding and well-respected members of this community and what you're suggesting is outrageous.'

Flynn kept quiet, sat back, and watched the couple's reactions.

Judith Black pulled on her husband's arm and he sat back down again. They looked to each other for support and Black put his arm around his wife. The niggling thing was that Flynn didn't think they were lying to him with their denials. Their expressions and body language signalled confusion, fear, and bewilderment and then finally anger. Unfortunately, he was pretty sure the Blacks were telling the truth.

Flynn was startled out of his reverie by a motorbike revving outside the house and then the back wheel spitting gravel as it raced off. This time it was Flynn who stood. Looking out of the window he caught sight of it being ridden away.

He whirled around. 'Who was that?'

'It's only our son,' said John.

'Does he work in the firm?'

'Yes, why?'

'What is his job?' Flynn demanded.

Black frowned but said, 'He obtains any planning permission we need.'

Judith Black nodded in agreement with her husband.

'Is he good at it?'

'Very. He's not let me down yet. It's quite a complex process, but training Ollie up has saved us a lot of money as we no longer need to use a professional planning advisor and town planning consultancy. They charge ridiculous fees. So Ollie gained experience as a Local Government Town Planner first and then came to work for the family firm. Bringing his valuable skills and contacts with him.'

Flynn wondered how Ollie had managed to not let his father down yet. What backroom deals had the boy been doing? Flynn scratched his face and then went cold. Dear God, what had he got wrong? Then it came to him.

'Mrs Black, where's your library card?'

'In my purse, it's just here.'

She leaned over the side of the settee, retrieved her handbag, picking her purse out of it. She opened the purse and then said, 'Oh, it's gone! Where on earth could it be?'

She began rifling through her purse, then her handbag.

'It's not here! I always keep it in my purse for when I pop into town.'

It was then Flynn realised he had made a terrible mistake and fled the house. As he ran to his car Mr and Mrs Black called out to him, but he ignored them and threw himself inside and turned on the engine. As he drove, he tried repeatedly to call Mabel's mobile but without success. She simply wasn't picking up.

Chapter 24

Mabel had just settled herself next to her friend, patted the hand of the patient and put her bag of grapes on top of the patient's locker, when another person joined them at the bedside.

'Oh, Ollie, how nice to see you,' said Mrs Prior. Turning to Mabel she explained, 'Ollie was at school with our son, you know. Stayed firm friends, haven't you?'

'Yes, and I hope I'm a close friend of the family, not just of Cameron's.'

'Oh, of course, you are.'

'How's Mr Prior doing?' asked Ollie. 'I was passing, and thought I'd just pop in. I'd heard about him being in hospital, so I wanted to pass on my regards and best wishes for a speedy recovery.'

'The doctor said the operation went well, so fingers crossed, eh?'

'Indeed. Look, ladies, why don't you go and grab a coffee? I'll sit with Mr Prior a while,' he offered. 'He's sleeping anyway, so I'm sure he won't miss you.'

'That's very kind of you, Ollie. Come on, Mabel, I've been dying for a coffee for an hour or more.'

'Oh, do you think we should?' said Mabel, not wanting to leave her post and upset Flynn.

'Please, Mabel, don't be difficult, come on,' and Mrs Prior scraped back her chair and stood, clearly determined to get her coffee.

Thinking quickly, Mabel realised she could sit

in the café which was next to the main doors and see everyone coming and going. It was the best she could do under the circumstances and still keep a vigilant eye out for the man Flynn was expecting to appear. So she followed her friend out of the ward, albeit reluctantly.

As Mabel and Mrs Prior emerged from the lift on the ground floor, she spied Flynn rushing in through the hospital main doors.

'Order me a tea, would you?' she asked Mrs Prior and went to speak to Flynn.

'What are you doing here?' he demanded. 'Why aren't you at Mr Prior's bedside like I asked?'

'We just came down for coffee,' explained Mabel, wondering why Flynn was in such a flap. 'Mrs Prior insisted. There wasn't much I could do about it, Flynn.'

'But what about Mr Prior?'

Mrs Prior joined them then and said, 'Hello, Sgt Flynn. Oh, he's fine. Cameron's old school friend Ollie has come to visit. We are his home from home, didn't you know? We are more like one big family really. The two firms have been working together for years. Anyway I came to ask if you wanted a cake, Mabel? They have some rather nice-looking muffins.'

'Who?' said Flynn looking from one woman to the other.

'Mrs Prior, dear, what's Ollie's surname? Mabel asked.

'Why it's Black. Ollie Black. Didn't you know

that? I thought everyone knew the Blacks.'

As the penny dropped, Mabel said, 'Oh my, Flynn. What have I done?'

Ignoring her and whirling around, Flynn didn't wait for Mabel, but ran towards the lifts. Finding both of them on upper floors, he barged through the doors to the stairwell. As be bounded up the concrete steps, for once he was glad of the hills around Muddlebay. All that walking up and down them had done his leg muscles good he decided as he climbed up three flights of stairs without so much as a twinge.

Entering the ward, he grabbed a nurse. 'Police. Which bed is Mr Prior in?'

'The last on the left. But he's already got a visitor.'

Running down the ward, oblivious to the cries of the staff telling him to stop, he skidded to a halt near Prior's bed. The curtains were closed.

Not a god sign.

Flynn grabbed the nearest one and with one good pull yanked it off its rails, to reveal Ollie Black holding a pillow over Ian Prior's face. While he still had the element of surprise, Flynn barrelled into Ollie Black, in a tackle that any rugby player would have been proud of.

Chapter 25

For once Flynn was really happy to return to Muddlebay police station, as he walked through the door with Ollie Black in handcuffs. The looks on the faces of Elgin and Fisher were something Flynn would savour for quite a while.

'Ah, there you are, Sgt Fisher,' Flynn called. 'Book young Ollie Black here in, would you?'

Fisher seemed incapable of speech, his mouth flapping open and shut made him look gormless.

'What's the charge?' Elgin asked.

'Attempted murder, for now, but I've no doubt there'll be other charges once I've interviewed him, eh, Ollie?'

Ollie Black didn't respond to that, just glowered at Flynn.

'Attempted murder?' Fisher spluttered. 'But this is Ollie Black you're talking about. That can't be right surely.'

'Attempted murder of who?' asked Elgin.

'Ian Prior.'

'You must be wrong! Nothing ever happens in Muddlebay!' said Elgin.

'Especially not murder,' said Fisher.

'Well it does now. Or maybe in the past it did but you just didn't notice? Either way, book young Ollie in while Elgin goes and gets me a rather nice coffee from the café on the High Street.'

'What about me? Can I have a hot chocolate?' At

a glare from Flynn, Ollie mumbled, 'I guess not,' and shuffled after Sgt Fisher.

It was fifteen minutes later when Flynn joined Ollie in the interview room.

'Can't you take these cuffs off?'

'No,' answered Flynn.

'But…'

'Don't whine,' he snapped. 'Right, let's get on with it.'

But Flynn didn't get any further before the door to the interview room was opened and in stepped a gentleman in a jet-black suit, carrying a leather briefcase.

'Oh dear,' he said, placing his briefcase on the table. 'I hope you've not started interviewing my client before he's had a chance to speak to his legal representative.'

'And who are you?' Flynn said, his face burning, for of course that was what he had intended to do.

'Giles Dawson, Mr Black's solicitor. Now if you don't mind?'

Reluctantly Flynn got up and took the card the solicitor held out to him. Turning towards the door he was called back.

'The handcuffs please? Let's get them off.'

Grinding his teeth to stop himself saying something he'd regret later, Flynn fished in his pocket for the keys to the handcuffs and removed them from Ollie Black's wrists.

'Thank you,' said Dawson with some satisfaction. 'I'll let you know when we're ready,' and shooed Flynn outside, shutting the door firmly behind him.

Chapter 26

But, of course, his solicitor appearing was only a short reprieve for young Ollie Black, for Flynn was an eyewitness to attempted murder. And neither Black, nor his solicitor, could stop him. Or at least that was what Flynn told Mabel over a welcome cup of tea in her snug living room the next day.

'So this is what I think happened. Ollie Black had wanted to impress his father by bringing in the planning permission for the six bungalows,' explained Flynn. 'He had half of the planning committee agreeing, but once again the casting vote would have been Mayor Carter, and despite Ollie's best attempts at persuasion, he'd refused to consider voting in Blacknote's favour, so he had to go. Ollie would then install a new mayor, who would be more amenable to their plans and ensure the success of future developments.'

'Tom Ludlow.'

'Yes.'

Mabel paused, an all-butter shortbread finger halfway to her mouth. 'But why him? He voted against Blacknote last time, didn't he? When the plans specified houses?'

'I reckon Ollie urged Ludlow to remember which side his bread was buttered on. He regularly took back handers from Blacknote, apparently, and that's why Ollie couldn't understand why Ludlow had voted against the plans for six houses. But Ludlow told Ollie that if they changed the buildings to bungalows, he'd vote for the development next time around.'

'What sort of back handers? Money?'

'Oh, not money, that would be too obvious. Holidays, weekends away, a new extension at cost price, that sort of thing. I think they saw it as more an old boy's network than taking bribes.'

Mabel nodded. 'Like the Masons.'

'I suppose. I don't know anything about the Masons. Where do they live? Are they a local family?'

'Let's go back to Mayor Carter,' said Mabel quickly. 'How did Ollie come up with the poison? Here, have a finger,' and she picked up the plate of biscuits and offered it to Flynn.

Taking one, Flynn said, 'He knew the Mayor was on atropine for his heart condition, and so hoped he would have some port and then an overdose of atropine from the Deadly Nightshade would kill him but look like an accidental overdose.' Flynn ate half the shortbread.

He was just about to pop the remainder into his mouth, when Mabel said, 'Yes, but how did he find out about Deadly Nightshade? He hadn't borrowed any books on poisons from the library. Had he searched that Google thingy?'

'Ah, well,' Flynn waved the biscuit around to add emphasis to his words. 'He thought he was being clever by concealing his tracks. He didn't do an internet search, which could leave a footprint on his account. So he used his mother's library card to borrow a book on poisonous plants and then recognised Deadly Nightshade as something growing on a small part of the plot.'

'Just like I did,' said Mabel. 'Flynn, are you going to eat that biscuit or play with it.'

'What?' Flynn wasn't sure how one played with biscuits and he looked at the shortbread finger from all angles in case he'd missed something.

'Oh never mind,' said Mabel. 'Back to the case. How did Ollie know the port would go to the Mayor?'

Flynn put the half-eaten biscuit into the saucer of his teacup and dusted the sugar off his hands. 'The most likely scenario is that Ollie secretly placed the bottles on the shelf in Prior's office, then casually asked Prior if he liked port, as he had some. Prior confessed he didn't like the stuff and didn't know where the bottles had come from, which we already knew, and Black suggested that as the Mayor liked port, how about donating them to him? To which Prior readily agreed.'

'But he didn't give the doctored port to the Mayor, did he?'

'No. He gave them to Tom Ludlow. And that's when Ludlow passed one onto the Mayor, keeping one for himself. And, of course, Ollie overheard me talking to his parents, saying that Prior was in hospital and had been helping me with my enquiries and that I thought the port had been doctored. As we agreed, I said that I was confident Prior would give me the name of the person who had handed him the doctored port when he came round from the anaesthetic and that's when Ollie decided Prior had to be stopped. He needed to shut Prior up as he could have ruined everything.'

'Yes, but in the end, Ollie managed to ruin everything all by himself.'

'Exactly, as in the old adage, crime doesn't pay.'

Chapter 27

However, the next day, Ollie Black had the last laugh, or so it seemed to Flynn. It was the hearing at Muddlebay Magistrates Court, where Ollie would have to answer to the charge. Sat at the back of the courtroom, Flynn looked Ollie up and down. His face had a five o'clock shadow, his shirt was rumpled, and his shoes had no laces in them. Someone, quite possibly his mother, had given him a jacket to wear, but in all honesty, it didn't go well with his grubby jeans. And coming from Flynn, who had no clothes sense whatsoever, well, that was an indication as to how awful Ollie Black looked.

Both his parents sat in the row behind and next to him lounged his solicitor, the ever-suave Giles Dawson. As the charge of attempted murder of Ian Prior was read out, his mother audibly gasped and dabbed at her eyes with a crumpled tissue. Flynn could see Ollie's father, John Black, tensing his jaw and flexing his hands, then bunching them into fists. Who Black was so annoyed with wasn't clear, it could be his son or even the police. Either way Flynn intended to keep well away from him.

'Would the defendant please stand,' intoned the Magistrate. 'Ollie Black, you are charged with the attempted murder of Ian Prior. How do you plead? Guilty or not guilty?'

'Not guilty,' Ollie replied. It was Flynn's turn to gasp. He was so sure of his case that he had never contemplated that Ollie Black would plead not guilty. Let's face it, it wasn't often that a killer was stopped by a policeman in the act. Flynn had burst in on Ollie trying to suffocate Ian Prior with a pillow. Flynn couldn't think of a better witness to a crime than a policeman. He was aghast at the injustice and could feel the pressure in his head building so much it felt fit to burst and he had to take several deep breaths to calm himself down. He couldn't abide liars and lies, which is probably why he was so tenacious as a policeman. He loved nothing better than routing them out. But several deep breaths later, thinking about it logically, a 'not guilty' plea was exactly what anyone with their head screwed on would have done. Still, the thought of a protracted case at the Crown Court didn't please Flynn. He had been looking forward to a successful prosecution and as a result leaving Muddlebay and returning to London, his exile over. But it looked like DCI Stride would have an ongoing prosecution as a good excuse to keep Flynn in his hometown and as far away from the Metropolitan Police as possible.

Glumly, Flynn listened as Giles Dawson was quick to ask about bail.

'Mr Proctor,' said the Magistrate, 'what say you?'

'We would request that the accused be remanded in custody, your honour.'

'Why?' the Magistrate leaned over his bench and peered at the CPS solicitor.

'Because of the seriousness of the charge and the fact that Mr Black would have the means to flee the country, sir. The family are, after all, of substantial means.'

'Mmm, and you, Mr Giles?'

'Sir, Mr Black is of good standing in the community, his parents have said Ollie would continue to live with them and that they would vouch for him.'

'Mmm,' said the magistrate. 'I'm leaning towards custody, I must admit. This is a case of attempted murder after all.'

Flynn looked on with bated breath. He cross his legs and then the fingers on both hands. Surely Ollie would be on his way to prison later in the day.

'But I'll grant bail if Mr Black surrenders his passport and wears an electronic tag.'

Flynn shoulder's sunk. He really should have known better. Magistrates could be easily swayed, especially when it came to saving the government a few pounds here and there by not filling up prisons unnecessarily. He felt like he was having the day from hell as he watched Ollie Black nod his head enthusiastically.

'That is acceptable to my client,' said Dawson as Ollie continued to nod his head, looking to Flynn like one of those nodding dogs that used to be so popular on the back shelf of cars. He idly wondered if he should get one for his classic Morris Traveller, but then remembered that being a shooting brake, it didn't have a rear shelf.

Proctor jumped up and was about to speak when the Magistrate held up his hand and said, 'Don't even think about it, Mr Proctor. I've made my decision.'

So the outcome was that Flynn slunk away, dejected, and Ollie Black was joyously reunited with his parents. As far as Flynn was concerned, the future wasn't looking quite as rosy as he'd imagined it would only 10 minutes before.

Chapter 28

The lawyer from the Crown Prosecution Service wasn't amused. Flynn could see it from the set of his lips, to the shaking of his head. He was a nondescript man who blended into the background. Didn't stand out. Pretty much looked like everyone else. White shirt, dark tie, dark suit, black shoes, thick black hair that never seemed to move. He looked more like a pen pusher than a lawyer for the prosecution, for there didn't seem to be an ounce of flamboyance in him. Oh, and he was called Smith to boot!

They were going through the Ollie Black murder case and it wasn't going well. The more annoyed Smith got, the worse Flynn felt, the more muddled and frustrated he became.

'Where's the forensic evidence?' Smith demanded.

'With the lab. Isn't it?'

'Don't you know?'

'Well no, actually, normally the forensic people handle that.'

'Where?'

'What?'

'Where are these people? You're not in London now, you know, DS Moran, where there are huge teams of people helping with an investigation.'

'No, I suppose not,' said Flynn forlornly looking down at his hands. He had been picking the skin at the side of his left thumb and it was red and sore. It just showed how upset he was. How anxious.

'I'm sure of it,' finished Smith. The lawyer stood. 'Can I leave all this with you? We just don't have enough forensic evidence at the minute, Sgt Moran. It's all circumstantial.'

'But Ollie's statement…'

'His lawyers are angling to have that thrown out.'

'What?' Flynn stood himself in outrage. 'He confessed!'

'There was only you present. No other people. There were not two officers in the interview room, as per procedure. You didn't video the interview and only did 1 audio recording, not two. And that was on your mobile phone.'

'But I couldn't find the equipment,' spluttered Flynn, who was beginning to realise that this case was far from a slam dunk.

'You should at least have had another officer with you,' said Smith as he threwh the files inside his briefcase and snapped it closed.

'You mean Fisher or Elgin?'

'Exactly.'

Flynn wasn't happy about that, as neither man liked him, which was precisely why he hadn't involved them in the first place.

But Smith was still talking. He clearly hadn't finished his assassination of Flynn's practice and procedure. 'Have you found the equipment yet?'

'Equipment?' Flynn wondered if Smith was still

talking about the recording equipment.

'Yes, equipment. You know, to make the poison with. Do you know how the poison was made? Where it was made? What other ingredients were needed, apart from Deadly Nightshade, if any?

'Oh,' was all that Flynn could manage. Surely it wasn't that he was a bad detective. It was just that he was on his own and not part of a much larger team of officers. He was used to a senior investigation officer overseeing everything, who would deal with all of this stuff. But as Flynn looked at the lawyer, who was acting like Flynn was something awful and smelly on his shoe, he realised he'd have to step up.

There was no one else to help him. Only Mabel and she was a civilian, albeit a very canny librarian. Oh well, Flynn thought, mentally dusting himself down. He had solved a murder. Now he just had to prove it.

Chapter 29

Flynn tried to be upbeat when he spoke to Mabel the next day.

'So, what you're saying is that in order to convict Ollie Black of the murder of Mayor Carter, you have to prove how the poison was made and where it was made. Then tie Ollie Black to it all,' she said. 'Otherwise, you have nothing. No case to answer.'

'That's right,' agreed Flynn. 'The only case I have at the moment is the attempted murder of Ian Prior and Ollie and his solicitor will argue that the act was not what it appeared to be.'

'Really?' breathed Mabel. 'The cheek of it. You know, this is just like one of those Agatha Christy novels.'

'How? I'm not Poirot, just as you are no Miss Marple. Really, Mabel, you do say the strangest things at times.'

Mabel looked askance, but kept quiet, so Flynn continued. 'All we know at the moment is that the port was doctored, and the poison was more than likely delivered by a syringe, as there were needle marks in the cap of the port. But I don't have the needle, or anything. In fact, I don't even know how the poison would have been made!'

'Didn't you do chemistry at school?' asked an astonished Mabel.

'Of course, but it wasn't my best subject.'

'Oh no, that was mathematics wasn't it?'

'Yes...' Flynn stared off into space. 'I'd have liked to do more with mathematics, you know.'

'I'm sure you would, but your education isn't the matter in hand.'

'What? Oh, no I suppose it's not.'

'I'm sure it's not. Now let's find out how to make the deadly nightshade plant into a poison. I'll see what I've got here in the library.'

'And I'll log onto google.'

'The perfect combination,' said Mabel.

'Let's hope so,' said Flynn, glad it seemed that there was to be no more talk about murder mystery stories. 'My job could depend on it.'

Chapter 30

Together, Flynn and Mabel had come up with two ways to produce the poison. The first involved crushing the berries to a pulp and placing them in a bottle of port, where they would fall to the bottom as sediment, but the poison would infuse into the port. This couldn't have been the method used, however, as someone would have noticed the seal was broken on the cap. Another method was to crush and distil the berries and leaves, and then inject the resulting liquid into the cap. This was looking favourite, but it meant that somewhere there was equipment that Ollie would have used. And Flynn had no idea where the hell that would be.

As a result, he had applied for, and got, a search warrant for the Black's home address, any outbuildings on the land, and their cars. He was looking for the equipment used to prepare the poison and hoped he wasn't too late, and that Ollie Black hadn't thrown it away somewhere completely unrelated to him.

And so, he was stood outside the Black's house, taking a quick break from searching their house, and gulping a weak cup of coffee from a paper cup. Mabel had wanted to be present, but she couldn't take the time off. That was probably a good thing, Flynn decided with hindsight. He couldn't give the Blacks any excuse to ask the court to dismiss any of the evidence they had found, because a civilian was involved.

The trouble was that they hadn't found much. Actually, they hadn't found anything at all. They couldn't even find Ollie's mobile phone, tablet or laptop. Flynn was frustrated beyond belief. The only good thing in all this debacle was that the planning permission for Blacknote Development's proposed build of six bungalows had been turned down. Still, life went on in Muddlebay and Tom Ludlow had been duly elected as Mayor and his wife had been spotted shopping for new hats. Ollie Black was behaving himself and adhering to his curfew of 8pm and logging in with the police station twice a week.

Muddlebay, therefore, seemed to be serenely sailing along on calm waters, but Flynn could feel the undercurrents. The Blacks hated him for what he'd accused their son of doing. Prior was furious with Ollie Black for trying to kill him and then having the temerity to plead not guilty to the charge. He was continuing his business association with Blacknote Developments mind, (he knew which way his bread was buttered after all) but had absolutely refused to let Ollie Black anywhere near him or his building plots.

Flynn's musings were interrupted by the forensic officer, Tyrone Hayles. 'Sorry, Flynn, nothing doing. I can't find any electronic equipment that is purported to belong to Ollie Black. I've seized his parent's devices, of course, but I'm not sure it will get us anywhere. He must have another location where he keeps his stuff.'

Flynn nodded and in a desultory tone asked, 'Have you searched the loft?' expecting that Tyrone had. It really was depressing, but what could he do?

'The loft?' Tyrone's tone of voice perked Flynn up. 'What loft? There's no upstairs. It's all vaulted ceilings. You don't get lofts in those, just lots of exposed beams.'

'The loft marked on the plans.'

'The plans?'

'Yes, I pulled a copy of the house plans that were submitted for planning permission and then for building regs. Didn't you?'

The forensic officer gulped. 'No. Why would I do that? It's not standard practice.'

'Standard practice or not, the plans are a matter of public record and they show a loft, accessed from a door in one of the bedrooms.'

'You got that plan here?'

'Yes, it's in my car.'

'Let's have a look at it then.'

Flynn grabbed the plan out of the car and laid it out on the roof of his Morris Traveller.

'Here it is,' he said to Tyrone, pointing to one of the bedrooms at the back of the house. 'Whose bedroom is that?'

Flynn looked at the officer, to find his face had gone pale and was nearly as white as his over-suit, which was particularly troubling as Tyrone was of mixed heritage. 'I reckon it's Ollie's bedroom.'

'Jesus,' breathed Flynn. 'Let's get up there.' He

grabbed an unopened packet containing new over-shoes and gloves and over-suit. He hopped on one foot and then the other as he struggled into the suit and then tied the hood around his face. At the front door he snapped on his gloves and slipped on the overshoes before hurrying into the house and up the stairs with Tyrone following him.

Once in Ollie's bedroom, Flynn compared the room with the plan. 'I reckon it's in the built-in wardrobe,' he said and flung open the double doors to reveal a full rail of clothes. 'Give me a hand,' he said to Tyrone and they began to lift out the hangers and place the clothes on the bed. That gave them access to a floor to ceiling, wooden panelled, back wall. But no door.

'Damn,' muttered Tyrone. 'Where the hell is it? and he walked into the wardrobe and started to examine the panels under the beam of his torch. But the examination with a torch revealed nothing, so Tyrone started tapping the wall at various places.

'Here, listen, Flynn,' Tyrone said. 'I reckon part of this wall is hollow, see?' and Tyrone began tapping once more. 'This one is a dull sound,' Tyrone demonstrated. 'But this, it's a much sharper sound.'

'Yes, there's definitely a hollow section behind this panelling,' agreed Flynn. 'But how the hell do we get it open? There's no clear door, nor a door handle.'

Flynn bashed the wall in frustration. He'd really had enough of this case. It was one thing after another. He turned away from the wall, stomping his way back into the bedroom.

'Flynn!' called Tyrone. 'Look!'

Flynn turned back and there was a section of the wall slowly opening. 'It must be one of those special mechanisms where you just press and voila, the door opens. Plus, we'd expected it to open inwards and it opens outwards.'

The wall had indeed opened, revealing a set of stairs. Flynn followed Tyrone up them, excitement mounting with each step. The stairs were cut from rough wood, and were without a covering of carpet. They led to a loft room, fully boarded out and with electricity points and lights. Tyrone pulled a cord to turn on the energy saving overhead lights, which gradually illuminated the space. And there it was. Ollie Black's lair. Flynn gasped as he took a slow look around. There was a desk, with a laptop on it and a mobile phone next to it. On another table they found a small set of weighing scales, with what looked like deadly nightshade berries and leaves, stored in a screw top jar. Next to it was a pestle and mortar and, on the corner, a small distillery.

Opening the drawers in the desk, Flynn found various supplies, including syringes and vials of what Flynn surmised to be Deadly Nightshade infusion.

'Gotcha,' said Flynn happily, handing the crime scene over to Tyrone to process. Flynn himself went back down the stairs, pulling out his own mobile to give Mabel the good news. In confidence, of course.

Chapter 31

The next day, on Ollie's mobile, Tyrone and his team found a number of phone calls to one number in particular, together with texts and messages, confessing love and devotion to an intimate partner. Further examination revealed that that number belonged to Chrissie Prior. There were also a number of incoming calls. One which was received by Ollie a few minutes after Flynn and Mabel had left Chrissie Prior, when they'd quizzed her about her dad. Flynn and Mabel had both seen Chrissie making a phone call and chewing her pencil in worry. It was clear now that she'd been ringing Ollie to warn him.

Flynn explained to Mabel that such an act smacked of perverting the course of justice and was just what he needed to hold over Chrissie Prior's head. 'Let's go and see what she's got to say for herself. I take it you're coming Mabel?'

'Too right, Flynn. Lead the way!'

Flynn thought Mabel was about to add, 'Tally ho!' as she was getting very excited and brandishing her umbrella. He had to duck out of the way a couple of times before they made it safely to the car.

As they settled themselves inside, Mabel said, 'Come on, Flynn. What are you waiting for? Let's get on!'

'Yes, Mabel,' he said and stifling a laugh, started the car and pulled away from the kerb.

They found Chrissie in the company office, looking very glum. She was staring into space, chin on hand, elbow on the desk. She wasn't crying, but her eyelids were suspiciously red.

'Hello, Chrissie dear,' said Mabel.

'Oh, oh, hello…' Chrissie stammered. 'Wh, what are you here for? Is, is there something else the matter?'

'No, not really,' said Flynn.

'We just wanted a chat, you know.'

'About?

'Ollie Black,' said Flynn.

'Oh, right.' Chrissie looked down at her desk. When she raised her head again, Flynn was horrified to see that she was indeed crying. He had enough trouble relating to women at the best of times, but a crying woman, no that was beyond him. He was very glad Mabel was with him.

'Now, now, dear,' said Mabel, moving to Chrissie's side. She picked up her hand and said, 'There's no need to cry.'

Chrissie sniffed and said, 'Yes, there is, Mrs Heggerty. He tried to kill my dad!'

'Why don't you tell us all about it. Here, here's a hanky. Now wipe your eyes.'

Chrissie did as Mabel asked, then sniffed and confessed that she'd been in a relationship with Ollie Black for some months, although she insisted she hadn't know of his plan to kill Mayor Carter. Nor of his plan to kill her father. Even though he was a thug.

'Who is a thug?' asked Flynn. 'Ollie?'

'What? No, no, not him. My dad! He gets drunk and gets into fights, belts my mum, you know, that sort of stuff. He's very strict and wants to know where I am all the time. He makes me work here in the office, when I wanted to go to college and train as a hairdresser.' She shuddered. 'I hate him most of the time, but what can I do?'

'Leave?' asked Mabel.

Chrissie sighed. 'Of course, I'd love to, but I can't leave mum alone with him. God knows what he might do to her. And she won't leave him! I was sort of hoping that if anything came of my relationship with Ollie, I could live with him and mum could have come with us. Or something like that anyway… Oh it's all such a mess!'

Under gentle questioning, Chrissie said that she saw Ollie as often as she could, even if it was only meeting up for a quickie. Flynn stopped her there. That was definitely too much information for him to even contemplate, and he quickly changed tack. It seemed the couple had met quite a few times at the building plot, which added weight to Mabel's argument that Ollie had seen deadly nightshade growing on the plot and had seized his opportunity.

'He certainly knew what it was,' Chrissie said. 'He showed it to me and told me to stay away from it and to definitely never eat the berries as they were poisonous.'

'But he never told you what he was planning to do with the stuff?' asked Flynn.

Chrissie shook her head. 'No, he never did. I'd have tried to stop him if he had, so maybe that's why he kept it quiet. The thing is, Sgt Moran, I might hate my dad, but he's my dad, innit? Doesn't mean to say Ollie could go around killing him!'

Flynn and Mabel thanked Chrissie for her time and Flynn asked if she'd come to the police station and make a formal statement. Chrissie nodded, but her eyes filled with tears again, and Flynn quickly left before she started crying.

Mabel mouthed, 'Coward,' at him as they left.

As Flynn settled in the driver's seat of his Morris Traveller, he pondered that it was finally beginning to look like Flynn could prove his case. It was all resting on Tyrone now, and the forensic report.

Chapter 32

When Flynn arrived back at the police station, he saw that, finally, the forensic report had arrived in his mailbox. Flynn pulled his laptop closer to him with shaking hands.

'You alright, Met?' asked Elgin, not unkindly, who must have noticed Flynn's demeanour.

Flynn had to give Fisher and Elgin their due. They'd been a lot more respectful of him since his arrest of Ollie Black. Something akin to grudging respect, at any rate. Either way, it was better than being teased the whole time.

'What? Oh yes, fine. It's just the report...'

'Yeah, I know.' Elgin swung round in his chair. 'Let's have it then. What does it say?'

Flynn clicked to open the document and skim read the conclusion. Ollie Black's fingerprints, DNA from hair follicles on his laptop and saliva on the pestle and mortar all pointed to him having pre-pared the poison. There were syringes with his fin-gerprints on them, and which had traces of the poi-son in them and even a couple of bottles of port that had been doctored. All found in the hidden-away loft.

'We've got him,' Flynn breathed. 'We've got him.'

'Well done, Met, good work,' said Elgin and slapped Flynn on the back, who flinched at the touch. 'Oh, sorry,' and Elgin shuffled away. 'Great re-sult though, eh?'

Flynn nodded and gave himself the satisfaction of grinning like a Cheshire cat, if only for a few moments. 'I must tell Mabel!' he cried and ran the short distance from the police station to the library.

He burst into the library through the double doors. 'We've got him!' he shouted to her, then, wondering why he'd not had a squeak, nor a yell, in response, he realised what he'd done. The library was full and everyone had turned to look at him, Mabel included. One customer in particular, an elderly gentleman of military bearing, hissed at Flynn. Flynn grimaced at his faux pau, after all he was in the library where silence was indeed golden, so he whispered, 'We've got him!' but it didn't have quite the same impact.

Stifling a laugh, Mabel took his arm and dragged him outside. 'We've got him?' she asked, undisguised pleasure in her voice.

Flynn nodded enthusiastically. 'He had a hidden loft. It was all there, Mabel. Distillery, deadly nightshade leaves and berries. The lot! And Flynn's fingerprints and DNA everywhere. We did it!'

'Indeed we did,' Mabel agreed and then said, with a twinkle in her eye, 'Oh, Flynn, I am glad I live in Muddlebay, because it's nice and quiet and nothing ever happens here!' and they both fell about laughing.

Especially Flynn, because, for once, he'd actually understood a joke.

THE END

Body at the Wedding

When a groom jilts his bride at the altar, there is outrage in Muddlebay. That is until his body is found. The bride's father is accused of the murder, as it becomes known that he wanted his daughter to marry a nearby landowner and not the local wide-boy.

But Mabel knows the family, who own a chain of betting shops, and she just can't believe the father would do anything like that. Not the man she knows.

But, as Flynn points out, how well do you really know people?

And what are they hiding behind their painted smiles?

The second instalment of DS Flynn Moran's experiences in Muddlebay is available from Amazon, in eBook, audio and paperback.

By Wendy Cartmell

Sgt Major Crane crime thrillers:

kindleunlimited

Crane and Anderson crime thrillers:

kindleunlimited

Emma Harrison mysteries

kindleunlimited

Supernatural suspense

kindleunlimited

All my books are in KINDLE UNLIMITED and available to purchase or borrow from Amazon by clicking the covers.

Printed in Great Britain
by Amazon

79031385R00068